COLLIE

TERRY ALBERT

Collie

Project Team
Editors: Matthew Haviland and Jaclyn Ix
Indexer: Elizabeth Walker
Designer: Angela Stanford
Series Designer: Mary Ann Kahn

TFH Publications®
President/CEO: Glen S. Axelrod
Executive Vice President: Mark E. Johnson
Publisher: Glen S. Axelrod
Associate Publisher: Stephanie Fornino

TFH Publications, Inc.®
One TFH Plaza
Third and Union Avenues
Neptune City, NJ 07753

Discovery Communications, Inc. Book Development Team: Marjorie Kaplan, President and General Manager, Animal Planet Media/Patrick Gates, President, Discovery Commerce/Elizabeth Bakacs, Vice President, Creative and Merchandising/Sue Perez-Jackson, Director, Licensing/Bridget Stoyko, Designer

Printed and bound in China

16 17 18 19 20 21 1 3 5 7 9 8 6 4 2

Library of Congress Cataloging-in-Publication Data
Names: Albert, Terry, 1951- author.
Title: Collie / Terry Albert.
Description: Neptune City, NJ : T.F.H. Publications, Inc., [2016] | Series:
  Animal planet. Dogs 101 | Includes bibliographical references and index.
Identifiers: LCCN 2015036493 | ISBN 9780793837397 (hardcover : alk. paper)
Subjects: LCSH: Collie--Juvenile literature.
Classification: LCC SF429.C6 A428 2016 | DDC 636.737/4--dc23 LC record available at http://lccn.loc.
gov/2015036493

This book has been published with the intent to provide accurate and authoritative information in regard to the subject matter within. While every reasonable precaution has been taken in preparation of this book, the author and publisher expressly disclaim responsibility for any errors, omissions, or adverse effects arising from the use or application of the information contained herein. The techniques and suggestions are used at the reader's discretion and are not to be considered a substitute for veterinary care. If you suspect a medical problem consult your veterinarian.

Note: In the interest of concise writing, "he" is used when referring to puppies and dogs unless the text is specifically referring to females or males. "She" is used when referring to people. However, the information contained herein is equally applicable to both sexes.

The Leader In Responsible Animal Care for Over 50 Years!®
www.tfh.com

CONTENTS

ORIGINS OF YOUR COLLIE

O ur love affair with Collies is partially due to our fascination with the stories of Lassie and Lad, who we read about when we were children. Once you have a Collie, you will realize he really is like the dogs in these books: loving, gentle, funny, and especially careful with and devoted to children. Your Collie will be a friend and an active playmate with everyone in your family, while also serving as an excellent watchdog, whether you want him to or not! Collies aren't just beautiful; they are also smart and capable workers. They've served generations of farmers as herding dogs, and served as sentry and search dogs in wartime. Welcome to the world of the Collie!

The Collie has a rich and interesting history. By looking at where Collies were first developed and the work they were bred to perform, we'll learn how a pet Collie fits into family life while still retaining the qualities that we've grown to love.

THE DEVELOPMENT OF THE DOG

The information we have about the history of domesticated dogs is being constantly updated as new discoveries continue to provide more accurate data. Although scientists have agreed in the past that dogs are descended from wolves, they now believe that those specific wolf ancestors are now extinct, and that

By looking into the work Collies were bred for, we'll learn how they've become family pets.

dogs may have evolved between 10,000 and 60,000 years ago in several parts of the world at the same time, including Asia, the Middle East, and Europe.

During this time, humans were still nomadic and were not yet raising their own food, animals, or crops. As they migrated, wolves followed them, eating the bones and waste that man left behind. The wolves, with their acute senses of smell and hearing, alerted the tribes to nearby predators and game that they then killed for food.

Humans and wolves lived side by side, each benefiting from the other's presence. Some wolves were probably eaten, but those who were the least threatening and fearful had litters of pups who grew up accepting their human neighbors. Over generations, the wolf's partnership with his human benefactors led to cooperative tracking, hunting, and guarding ventures.

When the agricultural revolution began, civilization evolved from hunting and gathering to more permanent settlements and agricultural communities. By this time, man was specifically breeding those wolves/dogs who were the least aggressive and displayed other desirable characteristics. The dogs became herders, draft animals, livestock guardians, and companions—in other words: domesticated.

THE COLLIE IN NORTHERN BRITAIN

Researchers think the original herding dogs in Northern Britain arrived with Roman conquerors in the first century CE. Bred with the Celtic dogs who already existed in the area, by the 16th to 18th centuries, the black "colley" dog was being used to herd cattle in Northern England and sheep in Scotland.

The colley was a working class dog owned by poor farmers and peasants. The dogs were of no interest to the upper class, so they were bred for their ability to herd and drive rather than their looks. The colley became an all-around assistant to farmers, butchers, and cattle drovers. He herded, protected, and drove cattle to the market in any kind of weather, and developed a harsh, weather-resistant double coat. The dogs worked closely with people, developing qualities that they retain today: intelligence, alertness, keen eyesight, versatility, athleticism, agility, loyalty, and a loud bark.

The original Collies were much smaller; they were 14 inches (35.6 cm) and up at the withers (shoulders) and weighed 20 to 50 pounds (9 to 22.7 kg). They had shorter legs and longer bodies than today's Collie. By the 20th century, the typical Collie was taller and heavier. There are several theories as to how the Collie got his name. The dogs were used for herding black-faced colley sheep, which is possibly why they were referred to as colley dogs. Another theory is that since most of the dogs were black, like coal, they were called "coalies." Welsh and other

Collies were first bred to be working class dogs and were owned by poor farmers and peasants.

Celtic languages were primarily spoken in Britain in the early centuries, and the Welsh word "coelio" meant "to be faithful and true." Ancient Britons may have named the Collie for this characteristic, since it certainly describes the breed well. By the end of the 19th century the Collie was called the "Highland Collie," "Highland Sheepdog," "Scotch Sheepdog," or "Scotch Colley."

It wasn't until the 1800s that dog breeding for specific characteristics began and separate breeds were developed. Like most dog breeds, Collies were mixed with other breeds, which has greatly influenced what they look like today. Most of this breeding was not documented, and exists as rumor rather than fact. An 1887 book titled *The Dogs of Great Britain, America, and Other Countries* details the Collie's "brilliant black coat...greatly aided by the cross with the Gordon Setter," which is a Scottish hunting dog. It is also thought that Greyhounds were used to develop and improve Smooth Collies. Russian wolfhounds (Borzoi) were also added to the mix. You can see the Borzoi influence today in the Collie's long, pointed nose, which started to appear in the early 1900s. At the same time, rumors circulated that Samoyeds and spitz dogs were crossed with Collies to introduce the white coloration.

THE COLLIE'S RISE IN POPULARITY IN EUROPE

The Collie's future changed dramatically in 1860, when the Birmingham National Dog Show Society held classes for herding dogs at their show. The Collie was entered as the "Scotch Sheepdog." Interest in the breed grew from there; by 1860, the Scotch Colley had a class of its own in the show.

The Kennel Club (in England) was formed in 1873, and 78 Sheepdogs and Scotch Colleys appeared in its first stud book in 1874. The categories included rough, smooth, and short-tailed (the Old English Sheepdog). In 1881, the English Collie Club was formed, and members wrote the first standard to define the characteristics of the breed.

During a visit to Scotland, Queen Victoria was impressed by the Collies she saw and brought several into her kennels. Some of her favorites were the white and Smooth Collies. Since anything that interested royalty was immediately mimicked by the masses, the Collie's popularity soared.

The English and European armed forces also widely used Collies in World War I. They worked as draft dogs and messengers, and performed sentinel duty on the front lines. They would announce an intruder but were considered unsuitable as guard dogs because they refused to attack anyone. The Germans bought Collies in England and exported them, training them to find wounded soldiers for the Red Cross. The Collies would stand over a wounded soldier and would not stop barking until help came, making good use of the voice they are so well known for. The English used Airedales and Collies for police work and tracking because the breeds were considered so intelligent.

You can see the influence of the Borzoi in the Collie's long, pointed nose.

THE COLLIE IN AMERICA

When early settlers brought colley dogs to America, they were primarily used for farming. They looked very much like the old farm-bred dogs of Scotland. Collies were first imported to the United States for showing and breeding purposes in the early 1870s, and they were immediately popular. East Coast fanciers began to import, breed, and show Collies, and eight Collies were entered in the first Westminster Kennel Club Dog Show in 1877. All were imported or bred

from imported parents, but there are no records to indicate their background. In 1878, 19 Collies were entered in the show, including two who were imported from Queen Victoria's Balmoral Kennels. They attracted a lot of attention, and Collies quickly gained popularity in the United States.

AMERICAN KENNEL CLUB RECOGNITION

The American Kennel Club (AKC) wasn't founded until 1884, and was set up as an association of dog clubs. The first AKC stud book was published in 1878, but Collies didn't appear in them until 1885. The first male Collie registered in America was named Black Shep, and the first female was named Bess. In the first group of dogs, colors were defined by an odd assortment of names: black-and-tan, black-and-white, tawny, tawny red, black, white-and-tan, sable, and sable-and-white.

The AKC recognized championships that were awarded before the organization was founded, and the first American Collie champion was a black-and-tan male who won in 1880, named Ch. Tweed II. The first female Collie champion was a sable named Ch. Lass O'Gowrie, who won in 1881.

The Collie Club of America (CCA) was founded in 1886 and was the second breed club to join the AKC. The club adopted the same breed standard as the

English Collie Club. The first Collies-only National Specialty Show was held in New York City in 1894.

THE COLLIE'S RISE IN POPULARITY IN THE US

One of the most well-known early Collie fanciers was J. Pierpont Morgan. He began breeding Collies in 1888 when he founded Cragston Kennels. He was able to afford top-quality dogs, and greatly influenced the popularity and development of the breed in this country. He continued showing Collies until 1907 when he retired from the breed and switched to Pekingese.

By the turn of the century, Collies were well established in the United States, and by 1905, they were the number one breed in AKC registrations.

HISTORY OF ROUGH AND SMOOTH COLLIES

Although no one knows for sure, it is assumed that Rough and Smooth Collies both descended from the same ancestors. Smooth Collies are shown alongside Roughs in artwork dating back to 1790. While Rough Collies were found in Scotland herding sheep, Smooths were popular cattle-droving dogs in Northern England. The smooth-coated Collie was better able to navigate the hilly and overgrown English countryside. Most Smooths were blue merle with blue eyes.

One of the most well-known early Collie fanciers was J. Pierpont Morgan.

In 1884, the first Smooth Collie champion in England was Ch. Guelt. Rough Collies were commonly bred with Smooths to increase the quality of the smooth variety, and many breeders who showed Roughs also had Smooths in their kennels.

Rough Collies became increasingly popular on both sides of the Atlantic, and although Smooths were also imported to America, there are very few records remaining. In the American standard, which was revised in 1897, Smooths weren't even mentioned. By the 1920s and 30s, Smooth Collies had all but disappeared in the United

Smooth Collies were added as a variety to the Collie Club of America's standard in 1943.

States. A few Smooths were still being shown in this country, but it wasn't until 1942 that the Collie Club of America approved Smooths as a variety of the breed. In 1943, both Smooth and Rough Collies were shown at the Westminster Kennel Club Dog Show. Smooths enjoyed a resurgence in popularity, and although they aren't currently as popular with the public as Roughs, there are many in the United States.

The "Smooth Collie" was named a separate breed in England in 1994, and interbreeding between the varieties is no longer allowed in that country. In the United States, the two varieties are interbred, and smooth- and rough-coated puppies are often born in the same litter.

COLLIE COLORS

The original Collies were black-and-white, black-and-tan, tricolor (black-and-white with tan accents), or blue merle. The first two colorations completely disappeared by the 1940s, but tricolor and blue merle dogs still exist today. Breeders preferred less white in the early years of the breed, to the point that a pure black-and-tan Collie was of more value than a white one. White markings on the chest, neck, feet, legs, and tail tip became more desirable in the 1870s, and by the turn of the century, a white blaze appeared on many Collies' faces. Today the white blaze is not required or penalized in the show ring.

THE ORIGIN OF TRICOLOR COLLIES

Today's tricolor Collies (black, tan, and white) are the closest to the original Collie coloration. It wasn't until the 1870s that the sable color became popular, and some attribute its development to crossbreeding with Irish Setters. Once they were introduced, sables took over the breed and remain the most popular color today.

THE ORIGIN OF BLUE MERLE COLLIES

Blue merle Collies were very common until the mid-1800s. The color fell out of favor when sables appeared on the scene, and was almost completely eliminated by the turn of the century. A few dedicated breeders, most notably J. Pierpont Morgan in the United States, kept the color from disappearing completely until it regained its popularity. Although there were clubs for blue merle Collie breeders in England, their popularity in America lagged behind even the black-and-tan and black-and-white Collies—colors that eventually disappeared altogether. The first blue merle champion in the United States was a smooth female, Ch. Clayton Countess, in 1906. The first rough-coated blue merle champion, Ch. Leabrook Enchantress, was named in 1909.

THE ORIGIN OF WHITE COLLIES

White Collies began to appear in the late 1800s but were not favored for herding because they blended in too well with the sheep. Some were the product of

Queen Victoria and Presidents Benjamin Harrison, Calvin Coolidge, and Lyndon B. Johnson all owned white Collies.

merle-to-merle breeding, which can produce deaf and blind puppies, so that was another strike against them. But this coloration became very popular; Queen Victoria and Presidents Benjamin Harrison and Calvin Coolidge all owned white Collies. At that time the dogs were all white with no color markings at all. In the 1920s, white or mostly white Collies were as popular as sable Collies, and white Collies were added to the breed standard in 1950. In 1964, President Lyndon B. Johnson had a white Collie named Blanco.

COLLIES IN POPULAR CULTURE

No history of the Collie would be complete without telling the story of the two famous Collies who helped make the breed one of the most popular in America for generations of children and adults.

Albert Payson Terhune released the book, *Lad: A Dog*, in 1919. An accomplished journalist, his stories were based on his own Collie, Lad, and were reprinted from articles that had appeared in various magazines. His loving tales about his Collie's intelligence, courage, and loyalty were a huge hit with the public, and more Collie and dog books followed. To date, *Lad: A Dog* has been reprinted 70-plus times and more than 1 million copies have been sold. The real Lad lived to be 16 years old and is buried on the grounds of Sunnybank, the Terhune family home, in Wayne Township, New Jersey. Although the house was condemned and torn down, today the site is a memorial to Lad and the Terhune legacy, and Collie lovers gather there every August.

Eric Knight, a newspaper reporter and Hollywood screenwriter, wrote the novel *Lassie Come Home*. He was born in Yorkshire, England, and moved to Pleasant Valley, Pennsylvania, where he and his wife raised Collies. Lassie's story started out as a short story that was published in 1938 in the *Saturday Evening Post*. Knight expanded it into the novel, which was published in 1940. Metro Goldwyn Mayer (MGM) made *Lassie Come Home* into a movie starring Roddy McDowall and Elizabeth Taylor (her first film role) in 1943. Five more Lassie films followed in the 1940s.

Meanwhile, the number of purebred Collies registered in the United States in the late 1940s increased from 3,000 to 18,400, no doubt because of the screen star's popularity. *Lassie* became a television series in 1954 and ran for 19 seasons, becoming one of the longest-running series in television history.

BEHIND THE SCENES: *LASSIE COME HOME*

Eric Knight modeled the main character in *Lassie Come Home* after his own tricolor Collie, Toots. He named the character Lassie because the Collie is a

The famous dog Lassie was a sable Collie.

Scottish breed, and Lassie is a variation of the Scottish word "lass," which means "female." The movie was to be shot in black and white, and a dog who was mostly black would not show up well on film, so MGM cast several sable Collies to fulfill the role of Lassie. The small dog who played Lassie's traveling companion in the movie was called Toots, in honor of Eric Knight's own Collie.

Back in the early 1940s, there were only three color cameras operating in Hollywood, and they were used on big-budget movies like *Gone With the Wind*, not lower-budget films like *Lassie Come Home*. But that changed when *Lassie* was filmed.

On the day that a scene of Lassie swimming across a river was to be filmed for the television series, the "star" Collies weren't performing well, so Rudd Weatherwax was invited to bring in his Collie, Pal, who had been waiting on the sidelines as a stand-in. The studio was testing a color camera down river from where the scene was being shot. As Pal began to swim, he drifted down the river and came out where the color camera was set up. The cameraman filmed Pal getting out of the water and dragging himself onto the bank. When the shot was shown to MGM cofounder Louis B. Mayer the next day, he decided the movie should be filmed in Technicolor, and Pal became Lassie. Fred Wilcox, the director, was quoted as saying, "Pal went in the water...but Lassie came out!"

COLLIES TODAY

The Collie's popularity has subsided over the last decade, much to the relief of Collie fanciers who worry about health problems that can result from careless breeding. Collies remain a popular family pet, and sable is still the most popular color. Although there aren't a lot of Collies working on ranches as sheepherders or cattle drovers, a number of Collie owners enjoy sports with their dogs, such as herding, agility, and competitive obedience. Collies make excellent therapy dogs, and Smooth Collies serve as assistance dogs for people with disabilities (a rough coat requires too much maintenance for this work).

The American Working Collie Association (AWCA) was founded in 1979 to preserve the Collie as a working breed, and continues to do so today by promoting fun and competitive activities for Collie owners. Group activities include herding, backpacking, search and rescue, drafting, carting, agility, and therapy visits. The AWCA was the first organization to start a herding program in 1983, and it was later used as the model for developing the AKC herding program.

The Collie Club of America (CCA) remains the AKC parent club for the breed, and supports the Collie Health Foundation, which identifies and supports research for common diseases in Collies. In the past few years, genetic markers have been identified for several diseases, and breeders now have tools to help

Genetic markers have been identified so breeders can eliminate common diseases in Collies.

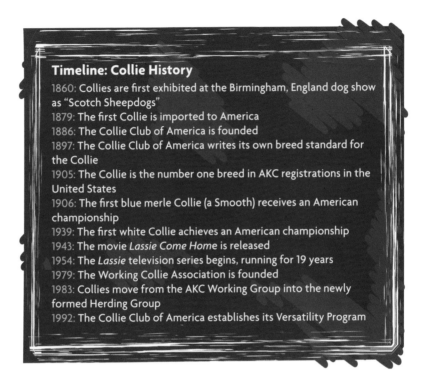

eliminate these conditions in the breed. The CCA also supports the Collie Rescue Foundation, which helps homeless Collies across the country and supports local Collie rescue groups. Almost every state has a Collie breed club that organizes conformation shows and companion events.

In 1992, the CCA established the Versatility Program, which recognizes dogs who achieve both conformation and performance titles. In the same year, the CCA began to offer a basic herding instinct test for Collies, and awards Herding Instinct Certificates to dogs who pass the test.

CHAPTER 2

CHARACTERISTICS
OF YOUR COLLIE

ollies are more than just a pretty face, and if you're thinking about adding one to your family, it's important that you learn about what it's like to live with and care for him. You and your new family member will be spending 10 to 15 years together, so meet some Collies and get to know them before you take the big step.

PHYSICAL CHARACTERISTICS

The Collie is an elegant dog, and everything about his structure and demeanor indicates strength, agility, and intelligence. The two varieties are Rough and Smooth, with Roughs being, by far, the most well-known variety. There is no difference between the two varieties other than the coat.

BODY

A Collie's body is bit longer than tall, but not overly so. He has a strong, level back and a deep chest. He is sturdy but fine-boned when compared to other breeds, which gives him a lithe, athletic profile. His relatively small, tight feet also contribute to his compact appearance.

The Collie's "tulip" ears are tipped over at the top.

PUPPY POINTER

A responsible breeder will interview you to be sure you'll provide a good home for one of her Collies. You will also want to ask her some questions and make a few observations:

- Are you allowed to meet the mother dog and the entire litter?
- Does the mother seem to have a nice temperament?
- Can you meet or see photos of the sire?
- Has the litter been raised indoors as part of the family?
- How have the puppies been socialized?
- Are all of the dogs in the home clean and well cared for?
- Does the breeder offer copies of health clearances for the puppy's parents?
- Does the breeder offer a written contract and/or guarantee?
  Here are some things your breeder may include in your puppy's going-home packet:
- sales contract, receipt, American Kennel Club (AKC) registration form
- record of shots and worming
- copies of the sire and dam's health clearances
- photos of the parents and a copy of their pedigrees
- blanket or towel that the puppies have been sleeping on
- bag of food the puppy has been eating

HEAD

Referred to as a "head breed," the structure of the Collie's head is very recognizable and important to breeders. From the side, the head is described as a blunt wedge, and has a very slight break at the eyes, called the "stop." Equally important is a Collie's expression—an indefinable quality, but one that truly describes his character. When you look into the eyes of a Collie, you will understand. Often described as a "gentle soul," a Collie seems to be pondering deep thoughts and asking you to share yours.

EARS

The Collie's "tulip" ears are tipped over about one-fourth of the way down from the top. They typically will tip naturally, but many Collies have fully erect ears throughout their lives with no dire consequences. The cup shape of the ear is ideally formed for catching and funneling sounds into the inner ear. In the early

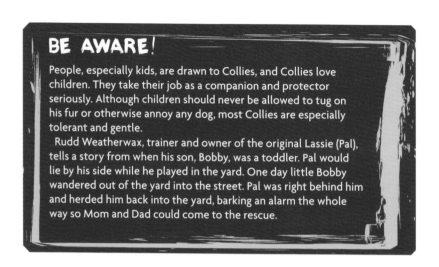

days of the breed, this was an important skill because he would be out at night on the moors, protecting the herd, and listening for approaching predators. The bend at the top kept out rain and snow, protecting the ear.

LIFESPAN

A Collie's life span is 12 to 14 years, although many have lived longer. The original Lassie, Pal, lived to be 18, and all but one of the Collies who played Lassie lived past 15.

SIZE

The Collie is a medium to large dog. Males stand 24 to 26 inches (61 to 66 cm) at the shoulders and weigh 60 to 75 pounds (27.2 to 34 kg). Females are a bit smaller; they measure 22 to 24 inches (55.9 to 61 cm) and weigh 50 to 65 pounds (22.7 to 29.5 kg). Most Collies fall into these ranges. They're not extremely strong and muscular like similar-sized breeds, such as a Rottweiler or Labrador. Collies don't seem as large because they have a light, somewhat narrow frame. They have a deep chest and stand tall and straight, which gives the impression of greater height. Collies have been described as large enough to demand authority, but agile enough to guide a runaway sheep back into the herd. Overall, the Collie is very easy to control despite his size.

COAT

The crowning glory of the Rough Collie is his glorious coat. Both the Smooth and Rough varieties have a thick double coat. Their undercoats are soft, woolly, and thick, developed to keep them warm. Their outercoat is harsh and straight, and repels rain, wind, and snow. The full frill on his chest helps protect the Collie's vulnerable neck from predators. The Rough Collie's outercoat is much longer and stands off of his body. The Smooth Collie's outercoat is short, harsh, and flat.

COLORS

Collies come in a variety of colors.

- A *sable-and-white* Collie's coat ranges from pale gold to deep mahogany. *Sable* Collies have white markings on their chest, legs, feet, and tip of their tail. Sometimes they will have a full white collar around their neck, and sometimes just a white patch on their chest. They may also have a white blaze on their face from forehead to nose.
- A *tricolor* Collie is black with the same white markings as a sable, but with tan shading on his head and legs. The tan shading ranges from pale gold to deep rust. While the original Collies were black-and-white, you will rarely, if ever, see a Collie without tan accents.
- *Blue merle* Collies are mottled grey or silver with black spots that can vary from very small dapples to large black patches. They also have the traditional white markings and tan shading of a tricolor. Blue merle Collies may have blue eyes, and either one or both eyes can be blue or partially blue. This has no effect

Collies come in a variety of colors, such as tricolor (left), blue merle (center), and sable (right).

on their vision; it's just different. Occasionally you will see an almost all-black Collie with just a small merle patch on his body, or a tricolor with a blue eye. These unusually colored dogs are called "cryptic merles." Be careful when purchasing a blue merle puppy. If a puppy is a product of merle-to-merle breeding, he may be blind or deaf.

Blue merle Collies have a mottled grey or silver coloring with black spots.

- *White* Collies are fairly rare, but perfectly normal and welcomed in the show ring. They are predominantly white with sable, tricolor, or blue merle markings on their head. Often referred to as a "color-headed white," a white Collie may also have color patches elsewhere on his body.
- There is another color recognized in Collies, but it isn't an official part of the Collie standard: The *sable merle* is a dappled sable Collie, and he may have one or two blue eyes or blue flecks in his eyes. This color is difficult to identify in a puppy's coat because sometimes it is very subtle. It is not a defect but a perfectly normal expression of merle genetics.

LIVING WITH A COLLIE

Living with a Collie can be a wonderful experience, as this breed has many positive attributes as a family dog.

PERSONALITY

Collies are known for their gentle nature and devotion to their families. When guarding a flock, they are fearless with predators and gentle with the sheep. A Collie is a good watchdog; he's an alarm barker, but you would have trouble getting him to bite an intruder. However, if that intruder runs, his herding instinct will take over, and he may give chase and nip her heels. Collies are not intense (like a Border Collie) or constantly busy, and they don't try to control everything going on in the household like an Australian Shepherd would. You probably won't catch your Collie herding the cat.

Some Collies do have a strong working drive, however. If you are looking for a dog who will be involved in herding, competitive obedience, or agility, work with a breeder to find a puppy who comes from dogs with that type of temperament. The American Working Collie Association (AWCA) is a good place to contact Collie owners who have working and performance dogs.

Males seem to be more rambunctious and more closely in tune with their owners. Females are more aloof and reserved. For example, when I was training my Collie, Emma, for snake avoidance, I had trouble reading her reaction and knowing if she recognized that a snake was hidden in a nearby pile of hay. She stood stock still and wouldn't walk forward toward the hay. Her lack of movement was her reaction. In contrast, my Labrador smelled the snake, put his head down, and took off in the opposite direction.

Collies are cautious but friendly. Because of their careful nature, you may find that your Collie is reserved when he's meeting new people. In the distant past, Smooth Collies had a reputation for having a more assertive temperament, since they needed to be forceful when driving cattle, but that has changed over the decades. Rough- and smooth-coated puppies are often born in the same litter, and there is no temperament difference between them.

Collies have a special bond with children.

COMPANIONABILITY

Collies are caregivers. Their reputation as family dogs is legendary, and many of those legends are actually true. Collies have a strong love for their people and make a loyal family member. They are not independent like a hound or working breed. The early Collies spent weeks with the shepherd as they worked side by side and kept each other company. They formed a close and loyal bond.

A Collie needs human companionship but not constant attention. He is happy to lie at your feet while you work or sleep at your bedside. Collies are approachable, not possessive or territorial. This is a good thing, because every time you take your Collie out in public, he will attract a lot of attention.

Collies have a special bond with children, are devoted to "their" kids, and are loving, patient companions. Like any dog, a Collie must be properly socialized and taught to behave around children, and children need to learn how to behave around a dog.

Collies might view children as small, darting vending machines. And when a Collie is up to no good, he's very quiet about it. As one Collie lover explains: "While we were watching an obedience match, a mother and her two boys came over to watch. Both kids had hotdogs in their hands. We said hello and went back to observing the dogs in the ring. While the rest of us weren't paying attention, my Collie, Jessie, daintily extracted the wieners from both buns. All of a sudden both kids started crying. When I looked and saw their buns were empty, I just laughed. Boy did we get a dirty look from their mom!"

Dog Tale

Collies have a legendary sense of responsibility for their people. According to Janet Merriman, a Collie owner from New Hampshire: "Once I was hiking Mt. Washington and my companion fell and broke his leg near the summit. I had to go for help and left my Collie, Seamus, with him. Seamus seemed to intuitively know my friend was hurt and lay down in the snow next to him to keep him warm until I got back with help. He normally wouldn't have wanted to leave me, but he understood and knew what his job was."

Monique Guerin, of Pine Grove, Pennsylvania, also relates: "When I am sad or ill, my Collies stick close to me, looking in my eyes for some sign that everything will be all right. A few years ago I had Lyme disease and was bedridden for a week. My dearest Farmer never left my bedside the entire time unless he was made to eat and go outside for breaks."

Collies have excellent relationships with other dogs, especially if they are spayed or neutered. The television Lassies always had a small dog companion, usually a terrier, who traveled with them on the road. It was a lonely life for the performing dog, and he needed a low-maintenance playmate. Collies don't have a terribly high prey drive; they live happily with cats if they are introduced properly and are not allowed to chase them. Bunnies, birds, and pocket pets, such as hamsters, mice, or lizards, may not be safe with any dog.

If you own more than one dog, the best combination is a male and female. Two females are more likely to fight, especially if they are related. Don't get littermates; that is a recipe for disaster when they reach maturity. Their temperaments are just too similar, and they will always be jockeying for position. The best scenario is to get one dog and wait at least six months before adding another to your household. Otherwise, they will grow up too dependent on each other and won't bond as well with you.

ENVIRONMENT

Just because Collies have a heavy coat doesn't mean they need to be outdoor dogs. In fact, just the opposite is true; a Collie will be miserable and unhappy unless he can be indoors with his family. Contrary to the romantic vision of Collies running across the Highlands herding sheep, they don't need large acreage or a lot of room to run. Yes, they got their start as farm dogs, but they are equally satisfied at home in a suburban house with a small yard, or even in an apartment.

Collies are very clean and fastidious. If they pick up dirt in the yard, you can easily brush it off the surface of the coat. Even when they're wet, they don't have a doggy odor. Their mouths are tight-lipped, so they don't drool like a Bloodhound or Newfoundland. Most Collies hate the water and won't want to swim in your pool. If he is introduced at a young enough age, yours might be an exception.

EXERCISE REQUIREMENTS

Leash walking is enough exercise for many Collies once they mature past the active puppy stage. Owners report that Collies have an on/off switch; when you're ready to run and play, they are too. If it's time to relax, they are the consummate couch potatoes. A Collie does need an occasional run at the dog park or a game of fetch in the backyard.

Collies will chase cars, bikes, and motorcycles. In fact, Pal, the original Lassie, was given up by his first owner because he wouldn't stop chasing motorcycles.

Dog Tale

Bob Weatherwax and his father, Rudd, owned and trained nine generations of Lassies for movies and television. They were asked if the Collie's temperament is suited to being a movie star. According to Bob: "We had to start training and socializing our Collies very young, because a lot of what Lassie had to do was contrary to his nature. The original Collies were bred to work alone out in the fields with the herd. They were wary and suspicious, always alert for sounds indicating predators that might attack the sheep. Collies today still might spook easily—not overly fearful, but cautious and sometimes aloof.

"Life on a television or movie set is chaotic. There are flashing lights, special effects like lightning and thunderstorms, cameras, hundreds of people moving around, and many things a normal dog never sees in his lifetime. To overcome this, we started bringing a future Lassie and his understudies to the set as puppies so that by the time they were two years old and ready to assume their role, they were used to encountering unusual sounds, objects, and people."

I asked Bob one last burning question: Did Timmy really fall in the well? He laughed out loud and said, "I don't know where that started, but there was never a well on the set, and Timmy never fell in one!"

The movement stimulates a Collie's herding instinct, and he'll run off in a flash. For this reason, keep your dog leashed in public.

TRAINABILITY

Collies are very smart and love the challenges that training offers. They were bred to work, and although they aren't as obsessive as some other herding breeds like Border Collies, they still need a job to do. As early as the 18th century the Collie was described as especially smart, with an "almost human-like intelligence" and a capacity to think for himself.

The lives of the sheep depended on the Collie's ability to make decisions and keep the herd safe, and he brings this ability and dedication to training. He wants to know that there is a reason for what he is doing, and will quickly get bored with repetitive tasks. Once he's done something right, move on to something else. You'll need to make training fun and fast-paced to keep your Collie interested. Harsh corrections will make him shut down and quit trying.

Overbreeding in the 1950s and 60s—Lassie's heyday—hurt the Collie's reputation. Many Collies were bred without regard to quality, and their health and temperament suffered. You may have heard the oft-repeated myth that their narrow heads meant they "had the brains bred out of them." That story goes back to the early 1900s when the breed (and narrower head) was still being developed, and flared up again when their popularity surged mid-century. Those days are long gone, and owners universally report that their Collies are extremely smart and love to be trained. Collies just think differently than other breeds, and you'll soon find they are quite clever.

SUPPLIES FOR YOUR COLLIE

The well-appointed Collie doesn't need a lot of accessories, but there are some must-haves for both Roughs and Smooths. You can go glam or stick with the basics.

BED

Some Collies won't use a bed, preferring to sleep on cool tile floors. Others are snugglers, and you'll find them endlessly fluffing and arranging their bed before daintily settling in for a nap. I can't help but picture a Collie on a fainting couch, one paw covering his eyes while he strikes an elegant pose.

There are probably as many types of beds as there are breeds of dogs, so you have a lot of choices. You may want to wait until after the chewing stage before you invest in a nice bed for your puppy. An adult Collie will need a bed about 36 inches (91.4 cm) long and 40 inches (101.6 cm) wide. This is an item with which you can make a real fashion statement. Find one with a removable, washable cover. Fabric choices include microsuede, denim, faux fur, or plush cotton. Pillow beds are stuffed with polyester fiberfill, cedar (to repel fleas), or foam rubber.

Wait until after your puppy is past the chewing stage to invest in a nice dog bed.

Bolster beds have a big roll around the edge on three sides to provide support. Wicker baskets have been a dog owner favorite for many years. If your Collie isn't tempted to chew on it, add a pillow. For senior dogs, a bed filled with an egg-crate-style foam rubber pad provides a soft cushion for old joints.

For use outside, consider a raised mesh bed made of PVC and waterproof fabric, similar to patio furniture. Raised about 8 inches (20.3 cm) off the ground, the bed allows air to circulate around the dog's body on hot days and is easily cleaned with a garden hose. Another hot weather option for your Collie is a cooler pad. Some styles are filled with water, and other styles need to be soaked in water for up to 30 minutes before use. Pads are made to fit most crate sizes.

CLEANUP SUPPLIES

Backyard cleanup chores will be much easier with a pooper scooper set, which is a long-handled rake or shovel and a scoop. Set up an empty 5-gallon (19-l) bucket with a trash bag in it to store waste. For indoor accidents, choose an enzymatic cleaner that removes urine odor completely. For cleaning up on walks, you can buy rolls of plastic bags to carry with you.

COLLARS

A rolled leather collar does the least damage to a Rough Collie's coat. A wide, flat collar will leave a path on the neck where his fur has rubbed off after a few months of wear, which doesn't matter unless you are entering him in dog shows. Flat collars can also cause matting in his coat. Smooths can wear any style collar with ease.

A head halter gives you more control when you walk your Collie. One strap goes behind his head while another fits over his muzzle. The leash attaches to the nose strap and you steer your dog like you would lead a horse wearing a halter. Some styles have an extra piece that attaches to the regular collar in case your Collie rubs off the halter. He can still eat, drink, and bark while wearing it. Because he can rub it off, a head halter shouldn't be left on a dog.

CRATE

An indispensable tool for the dog owner, the crate is your Collie's indoor doghouse. When you can't watch him every minute, he can rest in his crate and still be part of family activities. His crate is the canine equivalent of a den, and you'll often find him curled up in it with the door open. In his crate, he can safely stay in a hotel room or at the vet's office without a fuss. He has a safe place to get away from household guests or visiting workers. His crate is also a housetraining tool and helps you regulate his elimination schedule. Most Collies need a large crate, about 27 inches (68.6 cm) wide, 29 inches (73.7 cm) high, and 40 inches (101.6 cm) long.

If your vehicle is big enough for a crate, this is the safest way to transport your Collie. Some Collies are so stimulated by the passing cars, motorcycles, and bicycles that they bark and herd all over the car. The only way to stop this behavior is to crate your dog and maybe even put a blanket over it. This also helps prevent carsickness.

PLASTIC CRATES

Plastic crates have windows and a wire door so that the dog can see out, but it still confines dirt and hair. In warmer weather, plastic crates are too hot for car travel, but they are required for airline travel. The dog must be able to stand up, turn around, and lie down, so his crate needs to be pretty large. If you will be flying with your dog, check that the kennel is airline approved.

WIRE CRATES

Wire crates are another option. When I moved to California, I switched to wire crates because of the hot weather. While driving or at dog shows, wire crates allow for better air circulation. At home, your Collie won't feel as confined in a wire crate, and it may be easier to crate train him because he can see out. Some crates have a side door in addition to its front door, which

PUPPY POINTER

Wire crates are available with a moveable partition so that you can expand the space as your puppy grows. Puppies don't want to soil where they sleep, so confining him to a smaller area helps with housetraining. Never leave your puppy in the crate for more than four hours.

gives you greater flexibility in arranging your room. Heavy-gauge wire is sturdier, but the crate will also weigh more. Some canine boutiques offer crates with colorful wire and floral designs rather than plain bars.

MESH CRATES

Collapsible mesh crates also allow airflow in hot weather. They are so lightweight, they are easy to carry. The frame is usually PVC material covered with waterproof mesh fabric with zipper doors on top and at one end. Many have side pockets to store a leash or other supplies. These are a great option if you travel a lot with your Collie. A young dog still in the chewing stage may damage it, but mesh is a good choice for a crate-trained adult Collie.

WOOD CRATES

A wood crate is a furniture-quality accessory that deserves a prominent spot in your home décor. Often a less destructible, practical wire crate slips inside the wood exterior. Wood crates make great end tables and add functional beauty to your Collie's living quarters.

FOOD AND WATER BOWLS

Your breeder will probably send you home with some food so that your puppy won't get a digestive upset from suddenly switching brands. If you are going to switch brands, buy another small bag of that brand so that you can make the switch gradually. Learn how to choose the right food for your Collie in Chapter 4.

Collies don't need a huge bowl for their food. Although they are fairly large dogs, they are often dainty eaters. I prefer stainless steel bowls with a rubber bottom so they won't slide around the floor while the dog tries to eat. Stainless steel is also easier to clean and sterilize than plastic. Once a plastic bowl gets some chew marks on the edges, it looks shabby and is hard to clean. Ceramic bowls are decorative but break easily.

Ant-proof bowls have a moat around the food compartment that you fill with soapy water. For outdoor water, you might want to try a faucet attachment that

Stainless steel bowls are easier to clean and sterilize than plastic bowls.

the dog licks to get fresh water. He'll have to be trained to use it, but his water will always be fresh. A disadvantage is that you won't know how much water he's drinking or recognize if the faucet attachment malfunctions.

GATE

Pet gates are a must for training puppies but are also handy for containing adult dogs. For a puppy, housetraining is faster when he is contained and can't disappear into another room where you won't catch him eliminating.

Gates range from simple to fancy and budget friendly to high end. Simple gates are pressure mounted in the doorway and must be removed for you to pass through. More elaborate gates have an easy-to-open door that leaves the main gate in place. Gates come in simple wood and mesh, decorative wood, or metal to match your décor. Some can be permanently mounted in the doorway with screws. Extra-wide, freestanding gates block large passages.

GROOMING SUPPLIES

To keep your Collie clean and neat, you'll need a pin brush, slicker brush, undercoat rake, coat conditioner, toenail clippers or a rotary nail grinder, styptic powder, and dog shampoo. In addition, a Smooth Collie owner may want to get a shedding blade or shedding tool. For instructions about using these tools, read Chapter 5.

Oral care should also be part of your grooming routine. Use a doggy toothbrush and edible toothpaste. Toothpaste meant for humans can make a dog sick.

INDENTIFICATION

Every dog, no matter how well confined, could get out someday. If someone picks him up and takes him to a shelter in the next town, he may be euthanized before you find him. An ID tag, license, and microchip are his tickets home.

BE AWARE!
Make sure that the microchip you buy is International Organization for Standardization (ISO) compliant so that any local veterinarian, shelter, or rescue group can identify your dog. Most microchip scanners can read any brand or frequency throughout the world.

ID TAGS AND LICENSE

Consider putting your cell phone number on the tag so that whoever finds him can find you even if you are traveling. Tags come in a variety of fun shapes and colors: dog bones, hearts, stars, and more. Plastic

Put your cell phone number on your Collie's ID tag so that whoever finds him can contact you if he flees.

identification tags don't last long. The numbers wear off and they break easily as they age. Metal tags have your information stamped or engraved on them and don't wear down as quickly.

Sometimes a tag will get tangled in a Rough Collie's fur. To prevent this, you may want to get a tag that slips over a flat collar and lays flat against it. Custom-made collars are also available; these have your name and phone number printed directly on the collar. Fabric tag holders are another option. They hold all the tags together in one small packet.

Animal control agencies will often go out of their way to contact a licensed dog's owners, and some even offer a free ride home. Check with your city or county for licensing requirements. Licenses are always less expensive for altered (spayed or neutered) dogs. You may be able to buy a multi-year or permanent license, depending on what is offered in your area.

If your dog loses his collar and tags, there is no way for the finder to identify him. For permanent backup identification, have your Collie microchipped, which can be done when a puppy is still very young.

SUPPLIES FOR YOUR COLLIE

MICROCHIP

A microchip is a small computer chip no larger than a grain of rice that is implanted between your dog's shoulder blades. When a shelter or vet's office runs the microchip scanner over the dog, it reads the chip, just like a bar code scanner in the supermarket. The shelter can then trace the owner through a national registry. It is the owner's responsibility to register her dog's chip with the national registry, which usually charges a nominal fee for lifetime registration. Check with your local animal control agency to see which registry it is using.

Older microchips sometimes migrate down the dog's shoulder or leg. Newer chips have a hook that helps keep the microchip in place. Shelters usually know to scan the dog's entire body when searching for a chip. Have your veterinarian scan your dog during his annual checkup to confirm that the chip is still in place and functioning.

DOG GPS

A recent development in dog identification is a GPS system for dogs. A small device is attached to the dog's collar that interacts with satellite and cell phone towers to locate and track the dog's movements. You'll receive an e-mail or text message if your dog leaves the designated safe area that you have set up.

LEASH

Here's your opportunity to make a fashion statement complete with bling. Nylon leashes can be plain, patterned, jeweled, or neon. I prefer a leather leash because

Dog Tale

Liz Palika has been teaching obedience classes for more than 25 years in Vista, California. She is a charter member of the International Association of Canine Professionals (IACP) and is a Certified Dog Trainer (CDT) through that organization. She is also an American Kennel Club (AKC) Canine Good Citizen Evaluator and a Certified Behavioral Consultant. She was asked about using retractable leashes with Collies and provided this advice: "Never, ever, for any dog. They are dangerous. They can amputate fingers (this happened to one of my students), and the owner has no control when the dog is a distance away. Retractable leashes teach the dog to pull; the dog pulls, and the owner rewards the dog by giving him more lead."

it is easier on my hands, and the leather softens further with use. Cotton rope, similar to a horse lead, is another comfortable option, and these also are available in many fun patterns and colors.

Because Collies are tall dogs, I find a 4-foot (1.2-m) leash is best for most outings once the dog is trained. For training, I recommend a 6-foot (1.8-m) leash. During training you are practicing the *stay* command or the *recall*, so a longer leash comes in handy. When walking, you'll both get tangled up in a longer leash. By the time your dog gets 6 feet (1.8 m) away from you, he will be distracted and will start pulling.

Extendable leashes are awkward because the holder is bulky in your hand. The farther away your dog walks from you, the less control you have. Some of these leashes extend out 26 feet (7.9 m). If your Collie decides to take off after a squirrel or bicycle, he'll rip it right out of your hand. He'll also wrap you around trees and light posts. Unless you have a senior dog or one who is perfectly controlled, I don't recommend these leashes. Since most cities have a 6-foot (1.8-m) leash law, you could also get a citation.

TOYS

Some Collies couldn't care less about toys, but the ones who do love them seem to go nuts over stuffed squeaky toys. Buy the ones specially made

for dogs, and supervise your Collie so he doesn't open up the toy and eat the squeaker. If you buy stuffed animals at a garage sale for your dog, remove the eyes and other attached parts so your Collie won't chew them off and swallow them. The inside stuffing may not be safe to ingest. Many children's toys are imported, and the chemicals and materials used are not meant for dogs.

Collies often love to chase a flying disc, although you may have a hard time getting it back! An empty liter- or gallon-sized plastic bottle is an inexpensive and disposable toy that makes lots of noise.

Chew toys are a must for teething puppies, and most adult dogs enjoy them, too. There are a variety of synthetic chew toys and real bones. Synthetic (usually hard nylon) chew toys are cleaner in your house, whereas real bones, rawhides, bully sticks, hooves, horns, and marrowbones can splinter into sharp pieces. Supervise your dog when he has any chew toy, and remove it when it starts to break apart or gets too soft. Larger pieces are especially dangerous because, if swallowed, they can cause an obstruction in the bowel and require surgical removal.

Rope toys are great fun for Collies. They like to throw them around, shake them, and play tug of war. If bits are swallowed, the small threads can pass through the digestive tract easily. But again, when the rope starts to shred, you should throw it away. A big chunk of thread is as dangerous as a big chunk of bone.

Treat-filled toys are useful when you want to keep your dog occupied in his crate or when you aren't home. These hard rubber toys can be stuffed with peanut butter, biscuits, or bits of carrot, and they can be frozen until you need

COLLIE

them—or you can fill larger treat-dispensing balls with kibble. Your dog learns to roll the toy around so that it will dispense treats, thus keeping him entertained for long periods.

Put toys away when you can't supervise and until you can trust your Collie not to destroy and eat them.

WIRE EXERCISE PEN

A wire exercise pen (x-pen) keeps your Collie confined but still provides enough room for him to get up and move around. It is useful for times when you want him nearby but not in the middle of the action—for example, when you have company or you're at a picnic. X-pens are made of light wire and fold up for easy storage. They are available in 24-, 36-, and 48-inch (61-, 91.4-, and 121.9-cm) heights. Open it up into a circle and clip together the ends. Some x-pens have a gate.

Train your Collie to stay in the pen when he is a puppy, and as an adult he will be more likely to honor the boundaries. The x-pen isn't strong enough to confine a determined escape artist, so don't go off and leave your dog in one if you are going out.

A wire x-pen keeps your Collie confined, but still provides enough room for him to move around.

CHAPTER 4

FEEDING YOUR COLLIE

Sorting out the choices in the dog food aisle is a daunting experience, but you can make the best choice for your Collie with a little education. First, decide if your current food is working for your dog. If it is, there's no need to change.

Take a good look at your Collie. Does he look healthy overall? Are his eyes clear and bright? Is his coat healthy, or is it dull, greasy, or patchy? Is his skin healthy, or is it red and itchy? Does he have dandruff? Does he have normal bowel movements, or are they runny, bloody, too big, or too firm? Does he have constant gas? Does he have an appropriate amount of energy for his age?

Any of these problems could mean your Collie's food is not right for him. If you decide to change, there are guidelines you can follow when you make your selection. Remember, expensive food is not necessarily better, and no one food is perfect for every dog.

BASIC NUTRITION

To maintain good health, your Collie needs a balanced diet made up of these basic nutrients: carbohydrates, fats, minerals, protein, vitamins, and water, the most essential nutrient. The American Association of Feed Control Officials (AAFCO), the Food and Drug Administration (FDA), and the United States Department of Agriculture (USDA) regulate pet food manufacturing. Among them, they set standards that all pet food companies must follow in the production, labeling, and distribution of their foods. Although the basic nutrients and the percentages of these nutrients are specified, each pet food company uses different ingredients of varying quality. Sorting through the maze can get confusing.

CARBOHYDRATES

Carbs are sugars and starches that the body converts into glucose and uses for energy and various body functions. We usually think of grains, like wheat or corn, as the sole source of carbohydrates, but there are others. Simple carbs, found in fruits, are easily digested. Complex carbohydrates, found in grains, beans, and potatoes, provide starch and dietary fiber.

Whole grains, like oatmeal, brown rice, and whole wheat, retain their nutrients and are better for your Collie than refined grains. Refined grains, like white flour, have been stripped of vital nutrients like iron, B vitamins, and fiber. Companies use refined grains because they are less expensive than whole grains, while providing a good amount of calories. A dog easily converts refined grains to glucose, and thus, energy, so grains do provide some benefits.

Although most dogs are just fine on grain-based foods, some Collies have sensitive stomachs and have trouble digesting grains. You may decide to switch to a food with a different carbohydrate source to put less stress on your dog's digestive system. Examples of alternate sources of carbohydrates are potatoes, beans, apples, and peas.

Some manufacturers use fillers that provide no nutritional benefit, but add insoluble fiber to the diet. Examples of these "empty carbs" include cellulose or peanut hulls. Fiber helps the contents of the bowel form into a solid stool, but these fillers may contribute to excess gas.

FATS

Fats add flavor and texture to dog foods, and are usually sprayed onto dry food after cooking. Fat isn't necessarily a bad word; it provides calories (energy) and transports fat-soluble vitamins A, D, E, and K to the body. Fats assist in maintaining the heart and circulation, including blood clotting. Essential fatty acids lubricate your dog's joints and make his coat shine.

MINERALS

Minerals are the building blocks of your dog's body. Calcium helps build healthy bones and teeth. Calcium also works with phosphorus to aid in muscle contraction and other functions. Copper helps produce red blood cells, and iron is vital for supplying oxygen to the muscles. Zinc aids digestion. Iodine, manganese, and selenium are other vital minerals that support your dog's bodily functions. Your dog's food should supply all of the minerals he needs, and he shouldn't need any supplementation, except under the supervision of your veterinarian.

PROTEIN

Protein is a key ingredient in dog food and is often misunderstood. Proteins contain amino acids that build strong and healthy bones, skin, blood, muscles, and hair. The best proteins are meats (beef, lamb, etc.), poultry, fish, or other animal sources. Less expensive proteins come from plants and are used to increase protein levels in the food. They are named on the label as gluten—for example, wheat gluten or corn gluten. Dogs don't digest plant proteins as well as animal-based proteins.

Some dog foods have very little meat, and the meat they do include comes from poor-quality sources. When you look at a dog food label, look for a specific meat or meat meal as the first ingredient. Lamb or chicken is preferable to "meat." If not named, the meat used in the food could be different every time the manufacturer formulates a new batch.

Meat is mostly moisture, while meat meal is dehydrated meat and so contains more actual meat per pound (.45 kg). If you see meat as the first ingredient and corn gluten as the second ingredient, there may actually be more corn in the food, because meat loses its moisture in the cooking process. Look for meat meal or another animal protein source as the second or third ingredient if meat is listed first.

Avoid foods that use by-products. These low-cost ingredients are made up of feet, heads, beaks, intestines, or other parts, rather than actual animal tissue and bone. You have no way of knowing what is in the by-products

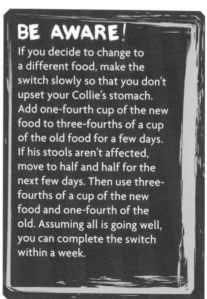

BE AWARE!

If you decide to change to a different food, make the switch slowly so that you don't upset your Collie's stomach. Add one-fourth cup of the new food to three-fourths of a cup of the old food for a few days. If his stools aren't affected, move to half and half for the next few days. Then use three-fourths of a cup of the new food and one-fourth of the old. Assuming all is going well, you can complete the switch within a week.

used in any particular bag of food, since it can vary from batch to batch.

VITAMINS

Vitamins metabolize and contribute to essential bodily functions. For example, vitamin A helps vision, and vitamin B_{12} is involved in nerve function and blood production. There are two types of vitamins: fat-soluble and water-soluble. The fat-soluble vitamins (A, D, E, and K) are stored in the liver, and excess amounts cannot be eliminated. The water-soluble vitamins (C and various B vitamins) are eliminated in the urine if the body has excessive amounts.

Vitamins are destroyed when exposed to heat, or due to age. Manufacturers add antioxidants or preservatives to keep the food fresh. Look for natural preservatives, like mixed tocopherols (vitamin E) or vitamin C. Synthetic preservatives, such as ethoxyquin, butylated hydroxytoluene (BHT), and butylated hydroxyanisole (BHA), are less desirable.

A complete food should provide all the vitamins your Collie needs so—as with minerals—you shouldn't have to supplement his diet in any way. In fact, an excess of some vitamins can be toxic.

WATER

Every function in the body depends on water. Dry food provides very little moisture, so it is critical that your dog has access to fresh water at all times. He will drink adequate amounts if the water is clean and fresh. Algae and other bacteria grow quickly, especially in warm weather, so change your Collie's water daily.

COMMERCIAL DOG FOODS

Commercially available dog foods are convenient for owners and work well for most Collies. The quality of these foods varies significantly. Evaluate your Collie's health, age, and activity level when you are deciding which one is the best choice.

There are many formulas to choose from that contain common or unique protein and carbohydrate sources, so you should be able to find a variety that meets your dog's needs.

DRY FOOD

Dry food is convenient compared to other options, and most dogs who eat it enjoy excellent health. Dry food is cooked—either baked or extruded. Some of the nutrients, like fats, are depleted by cooking, and must be replenished during the manufacturing process.

Prices vary from inexpensive grocery store brands to pricey premium foods that are available only at pet supply stores and boutiques. Investigate the ingredients list and choose a food with primarily animal protein sources.

Preservatives are added to the food to prevent spoilage and lengthen shelf life. As long as natural rather than synthetic preservatives are used, this isn't a disadvantage.

CANNED FOOD

Canned food is more expensive than dry food on a per-pound (.45 kg) basis, but there are many benefits to feeding your Collie wet food. The first is the moisture content. Most canned foods contain 78 percent moisture. The moisture content

Dry food is convenient compared to other options, and most dogs who eat it enjoy excellent health.

in canned food is similar to the amount a dog would get in raw foods. When your dog eats dry food he uses the water already in his system to digest his kibble. Canned food supplies the extra water he needs to properly metabolize his meal.

Most dogs drink enough water to stay healthy, and you can always add water to their dry food. But if your Collie is older and isn't getting enough water, or has trouble eating dry food, canned is a good alternative.

Canned food usually contains more meat, fish, or poultry (animal protein sources) than dry varieties. Therefore, it tastes and smells better to your dog and is easier for him to digest. A picky eater or sick dog will be more likely to eat wet food. Dogs do perfectly well eating dry and/or canned food, as long as you are careful not to overfeed. Cut back on his dry food if you are adding canned.

Preservatives aren't used in wet foods because the can is an oxygen-free environment; therefore, the food won't spoil until it is left open.

SEMI-MOIST FOOD

Semi-moist food is the most expensive, and is often made to look like sausage or beef chunks. Binders and grain glutens mold the ingredients into meat-like shapes, but the food may not contain any meat at all. Artificial flavors and coloring are added to make the food more appealing to you, the buyer. Some semi-moist foods have high sugar content, which damages your dog's teeth just like it causes tooth decay in people. Read the label to find out the actual ingredients. Many dog treats also fall into this category.

NONCOMMERCIAL FOODS

Dog owners have a variety of reasons for choosing to feed their pets raw or home-cooked diets. As mentioned earlier, many Collies have sensitive stomachs, and owners often find their dogs are much healthier when they eliminate certain ingredients and avoid processed foods. Other owners simply want to avoid many of the ingredients in commercial foods, such as grains, dyes, synthetic vitamins, and preservatives. In recent years there have been numerous pet food recalls due to contamination and inferior imported ingredients. People are cautious and want to be assured their Collie is eating safe, high-quality ingredients.

To get a proper balance of nutrients and supplemental vitamins and minerals, consider working with a veterinary nutritionist.

The benefits of raw or home-cooked diets include:
• The dog often has overall better health and attitude.
• Dogs with allergies tend to improve.
• You avoid processed food.

- If you buy organic or locally grown meat and produce, you can avoid pesticides and chemicals that are used on plants, as well as the antibiotics and growth hormones that are used in meat.
- Your Collie's stools will be smaller because he metabolizes food better and uses all the nutrients. There are also no fillers to contribute excess volume.
- You get to select the ingredients and develop a formula that works well for your dog.
- You don't have to feed your Collie 100 percent raw or home-cooked food; you can supplement it with a quality commercial food so that he still gets the vitamins and minerals he needs.

Drawbacks of raw or home-cooked diets include:

- They are more expensive.
- It is difficult to get the right balance of nutrients, vitamins, and minerals.
- It takes a lot of time and effort to plan, shop, and prepare the meals.
- There's a risk of using too much fat, which can cause pancreatitis, a potentially fatal disease.
- It is difficult to use raw or home-cooked foods if you are traveling with or boarding your dog.
- Cooked bones can splinter and perforate the bowel or intestine.
- Raw meat must be handled carefully to avoid spoilage and contamination with *E. coli* or *Salmonella*, which could make both you and your dog seriously ill.

RAW DIETS

Raw diets for dogs have been around for a number of years and have become so popular that there are now commercially made raw foods available. Referred to as BARF (Bones and Raw Food, or Biologically Appropriate Raw Food), owners prepare a combination of raw meat, fruits, vegetables, and supplements. Because the food is raw, all of the natural vitamins, minerals, and nutrients are retained. Proponents of raw feeding believe this is the most natural way to feed a dog and that this method is the closest to how his ancestors ate in the wild.

The most serious concern about raw feeding is the risk of contamination. Both humans and dogs can become ill from *E. coli* and *Salmonella* bacteria. You must be especially careful while handling and preparing raw foods; clean your countertops, knives, appliances, and dog dishes after every meal. If there are humans or dogs in your home with a compromised immune system, they should not be exposed to raw meat.

If you feed your dog raw bones, inspect his stool for bits of bone. It may be safer to grind the bones before feeding.

HOME-COOKED DIETS

Cooking removes some nutrients from food but not as much as the high-heat processing methods used in manufacturing plants. Owners who cook for their dogs usually make a stew of meats and vegetables. Cooked vegetables are easier for your dog to digest. Leftover ingredients from your own meals can also be used in your dog's diet, but beware; many of the seasonings and additives that you like could make your dog sick. Table scraps do not provide a balanced diet.

Trim large pieces of fat off of the meat before cooking. Too much fat can cause pancreatitis or other stomach upsets. Leftover turkey from holiday feasts is often the cause of pancreatitis in dogs, much to the horror of their well-meaning owners.

If you add any cooked bones to your Collie's diet, grind them completely before serving. Cooked bones are more dangerous than raw because they are dry and brittle. They easily splinter into dangerous shards.

FREE FEEDING VERSUS SCHEDULED FEEDING

Most adult dogs do better on two meals each day. If you feed him just once in the evening, for example, your Collie will be hungry all the next day while you are at work, and the resulting stress could cause him to be destructive. Set the food dish down and leave it for 15 minutes. If he doesn't eat, pick it up and save it for the next meal. Don't be tempted to add table scraps or canned food to tempt him; he'll quickly train you to feed him all kinds of junk he doesn't need.

FEEDING YOUR COLLIE

Try to feed him at the same times each day. Your Collie will know when to expect his meal, will experience less stress, and won't pester you to feed him at odd times.

Because most Collies don't overeat, you may think it's not important to feed your dog on a schedule. But there are some good reasons:

If you have more than one dog, free feeding is not a good idea, because it's hard to tell if one of the dogs is not eating.

- When you leave food out for him all day, you don't know how much your dog is eating. If he's not eating it will take you several days to figure it out.
- If you have more than one dog, you don't know who is eating and who isn't.
- Leaving food out attracts ants and flies, especially if it's canned food or if you add water.
- It's harder to regulate housetraining, because if you don't know when your dog has eaten, you don't know when he needs to go out.
- Leaving food out encourages picky eating.
- Dogs look to you as their providers. When you are training or playing with your Collie, you use food to motivate him. The food loses its value if it's always available.

PICKY EATER OR UNDERWEIGHT?

Many Collies are fussy eaters or just aren't too interested in food. If your dog misses an occasional meal, it isn't going to hurt him. Monitor his stools to be sure he isn't suffering from diarrhea or other stomach upset.

Stress will ruin a Collie's appetite. Consider what is going on in your home that may make him too anxious to eat. Are you packing for a trip? Has company come to visit? Has someone moved out? Is the family under stress that he can sense? Once his anxiety passes, he'll probably go back to his usual eating habits.

If your Collie chronically refuses to eat, you may want to try a food with a different protein source. For example, try lamb instead of chicken to see which he prefers. Don't be tempted to add table scraps, because you will create a picky eater.

You can tell by his body condition if he's too thin. A dog who is severely underweight may have a dry, scruffy-looking coat and maybe even lose some hair. Have your veterinarian check a stool sample for internal parasites and for an underlying health problem that may be causing the weight loss.

SENSITIVE STOMACH

Many Collies have stomach issues, often with an unknown cause. This problem may or may not be caused by food. W. Jean Dodds, DVM, founder and president of Hemopet and long-time researcher of canine health problems, reports that dogs' primary food allergies involve beef, corn, wheat, soy, eggs, or milk. Symptoms don't always occur immediately after eating an offending food. It is difficult to associate a dog's digestive issues with something he ate, because he could've ingested the offending food days ago.

Dr. Dodds states that most food sensitivities don't show up until an animal is around two years of age. Soft stools, gas, constipation, vomiting, or other symptoms may indicate food sensitivity. A newly available technology actually tests a dog's saliva to identify his food intolerances.

Experiment with different proteins, less fat, or grain-free foods to see if they improve your Collie's health. Try to choose a food with a single protein and a single grain source so that you know which ingredient is affecting your dog. A food with additional fiber may also aid your Collie's digestion. It takes several months for the changes to become noticeable; give a diet four to six months

PUPPY POINTER

Puppies metabolize their food differently than adult dogs. Feed your puppy three small meals a day until he is four months old, and gradually cut back until he is eating two meals a day at about six months of age. Some puppy foods have too much calcium, which promotes fast growth and is bad for large dogs. Bones that grow too fast will not be as strong and dense as slow-growing bones; therefore, the dog will be more prone to injury until he reaches full maturity. Switch him to adult food by the time he is eight to ten months old at the latest.

before you decide it isn't working. Owners report that their Collies also do well on a raw or home-cooked diet if they have digestive problems.

Remember that diet may not be the cause of your Collie's stomach problems. A complete workup by your veterinarian will help you identify and confirm a diagnosis.

Look for signs of food sensitivity in your Collie; you may need to change his diet.

OBESITY

If your Collie is a big eater, then you definitely don't want to leave food out for him, because he'll be overweight in no time. Once your puppy reaches adulthood, he doesn't need as much food as when he was growing. Switch him to adult food, and cut back his ration gradually to the amount he needs. You should still feed him two meals a day.

Senior Collies don't need as much food because they aren't as active. You may feel guilty cutting back because you think you are depriving him, but you should use these measures to keep your dog at a healthy weight.

WEIGHT CHECK

How can you tell if your Collie is too heavy or thin? For a Smooth Collie, you can do a visual and hands-on check. Stand back and look at your dog. Does he have a slight tuck-up behind his rib cage? Look down at your Collie from above. Is there a slight narrowing behind the rib cage? If the answer is yes to both, that's a good sign. Do a hands-on check to be sure.

For both Smooths and Roughs, the hands-on check includes laying your hands flat on either side of the rib cage. If you can find your dog's ribs with a little

Don Ironside has worked as an account representative in the pet food industry for more than 20 years, and has raised and shown dogs for 38 years. When asked about adding supplements to a Collie's food, he suggests the following: "If your dog is eating a good-quality commercial food, all the nutrients, vitamins, and minerals he needs are included in the food. Too much of a supplement may throw off the nutrient balance and cause health problems rather than solve them. A dog who is fed a raw or home-cooked diet may need additional supplements in order to provide complete nutrition."

effort, he isn't overweight. If you have to feel through a layer of flesh to find his ribs, he's a bit pudgy. If you can easily feel each rib, he is underweight.

On a Rough Collie, it may be hard to tell your dog's condition under that heavy coat, so the best way to check is to put your hands on him.

WEIGHT LOSS PLAN

Depending on your Collie's overall health, consult with your veterinarian about his diet. Have him weighed so that you can get an idea of how much weight he needs to lose. Your vet may want to run some tests to rule out health problems, such as hypothyroidism, which causes dogs to gain weight. Collies can sometimes develop this as they age.

Rather than just cut his ration drastically, cut back gradually, about one-fourth cup at a time. If you cut back too severely, his metabolism will slow down to compensate for the reduced amount. Add steamed green beans, carrots, broccoli, or other vegetables to help fill him up. Canned pumpkin (not pumpkin pie mix) is another option. The additional fiber will make him feel full.

Many brands offer a "light" formula food. With this type of food, you don't have to cut back the quantity of your dog's food, but you're still reducing his calorie intake. Your veterinarian may recommend switching him to a high-fiber, low-calorie prescription diet.

When considering your dog's diet, don't forget to count the treats. Too many cookies will sabotage your diet plans. Instead, use slices of cooked sweet potato or carrots. Also, a big dog doesn't need a huge biscuit. Break it into halves or quarters and give him a smaller piece.

Just like in people, exercise will help your Collie lose weight. You'll both benefit from daily walks or active games.

FEEDING YOUR COLLIE

GROOMING YOUR COLLIE

A Collie's big, luxurious coat is his shining glory, but it's not as hard to care for as it looks. Collies are very tidy dogs, and their double coats are dirt repellent. Surface grit brushes out easily. But to keep him healthy and gorgeous, he does need routine grooming care—especially regular brushing—to prevent mats.

WHY GROOMING IS IMPORTANT

While you groom your dog, you are able to check for problems, such as suspicious lumps or foxtails, prevent problems caused by mats or parasites, maintain his teeth and toenails, and spend time bonding with him, which is just as important. I spend Sunday nights on the floor in front of the TV grooming dogs and handing out treats. They line up for their turn and look forward to our time together.

GROOMING SUPPLIES

The well-dressed Collie doesn't need a lot of equipment to maintain his good looks, and the tools you purchase should last a lifetime.

- **Comb:** The comb should be wide- or medium-toothed metal; get at least one comb that is no wider than 3 or 4 inches (7.6 or 10.2 cm). Combs wider than that are awkward to handle in tight places.
- **Pin brush:** This is the main brush you can use for both rough and smooth coats. This brush has plastic or metal pins on a soft rubber flat backing, and a handle. It looks like a hairbrush but has pins instead of bristles.
- **Rubber curry:** A tool for the Smooth Collie, the curry is a round or oval rubber tool with flexible nubs, measuring about 1/2 inch (1.3 cm) long. The curry fits in the palm of your hand without a handle.
- **Scissors:** Blunt-tip grooming scissors and/or thinning shears can be used for trimming his feet, legs, and rear end.
- **Shampoo and conditioner rinse:** Dog shampoo is less harsh on the coat

A slicker brush comes in handy for getting rid of excess hair.

than human shampoo. Some conditioners are leave-in and save you the hassle of rinsing. Conditioner makes a rough coat easier to brush.

- **Shedding blade:** This metal piece (about 12 inches [30.5 cm] long), for Smooth Collies only, is serrated on one edge with rubber handles at each end. This only works on the surface of the coat and wouldn't be of use on a Rough Collie.
- **Shedding tool:** This fine-toothed rake or comb removes undercoat hair on Smooth Collies.
- **Slicker brush:** The fine metal pins on this brush are closer together than on a pin brush. The pins are on a flexible rubber backing. A slicker is rectangular and smaller than a pin brush.
- **Spray conditioner or tangle remover:** Some brands are specially made for grooming a dog's coat. You can also use horse mane and tail products or human hair conditioner. An alternative is plain water in a spray bottle.
- **Styptic powder:** If you accidentally cut into the quick while trimming your Collie's toenails, this stops the bleeding.
- **Toenail clippers or rotary grinding tool:** Guillotine-style clippers make a clean cut. Get extra blades because they dull quickly. A rotary grinding tool has a sandpaper-covered cylinder at the end that files down the nail.

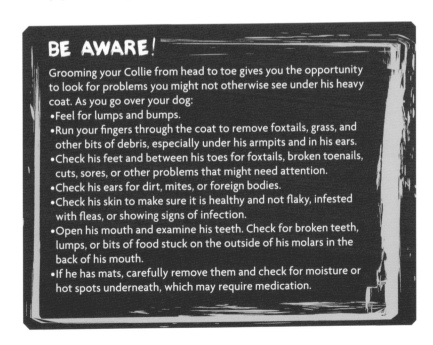

BE AWARE!

Grooming your Collie from head to toe gives you the opportunity to look for problems you might not otherwise see under his heavy coat. As you go over your dog:
- Feel for lumps and bumps.
- Run your fingers through the coat to remove foxtails, grass, and other bits of debris, especially under his armpits and in his ears.
- Check his feet and between his toes for foxtails, broken toenails, cuts, sores, or other problems that might need attention.
- Check his ears for dirt, mites, or foreign bodies.
- Check his skin to make sure it is healthy and not flaky, infested with fleas, or showing signs of infection.
- Open his mouth and examine his teeth. Check for broken teeth, lumps, or bits of food stuck on the outside of his molars in the back of his mouth.
- If he has mats, carefully remove them and check for moisture or hot spots underneath, which may require medication.

- **Toothpaste and toothbrush:** Dogs can't spit out toothpaste like humans do, so their toothpaste needs to be edible and is often available in meat flavors. Buy a fingertip toothbrush or a regular one with a handle. You can also get a rubber gum massager that fits over the end of your finger, or you can just use a piece of gauze.
- **Undercoat rake:** This wide rake with heavy tines set in a single row is for Rough Collies only. Regular brushes or shedding blades won't work for the Rough Collie's soft undercoat, which mats easily if it's not brushed properly.

BRUSHING

When you choose a Collie, you commit yourself to a regular grooming routine. Plan to groom him at least twice a week for about 20 minutes. This is an estimate based on a Collie who gets regular attention. If you brush often, it doesn't have to be a big chore. On the other hand, grooming a matted, dirty, rough-coated Collie is a daunting task. Don't put it off or you'll have health problems to deal with. Moisture gathers under mats against the skin and causes irritation, which leads to hot spots. Then your Collie starts chewing at the irritation and the mat gets worse. Bacteria invade the open skin and an infection takes hold. Now your dog doesn't just need grooming—he needs a trip to the vet and antibiotics.

Smooth Collies have fewer grooming needs than Rough Collies, but they still shed a lot.

HOW TO BRUSH YOUR COLLIE

All Collies, Rough or Smooth, have a double coat. The straight, outer guard hairs are longer and harsh to the touch. The soft, thick undercoat provides insulation to keep him warm in harsh winter weather and cool in the hot summer. On the Rough Collie, the undercoat is so thick that you'll have trouble finding his skin when you part his hair. The undercoat makes the outercoat stand out from the body, and gives our Roughs the lush look that we love so much. On Smooth Collies, the undercoat is not as plush.

Twice a year in the spring and fall, the undercoat of both the Rough and Smooth Collies sheds out. Like horses, they start to shed in late winter when the days get longer and there is more daylight, not because it is warmer. Collies who are indoors year-round will shed lightly all year because they are constantly exposed to a light source.

During these weeks you'll be dealing with masses of hair, and your Collie will need help getting rid of it. Groom him outside to make the cleanup easier. During shedding season, the undercoat rake will get a real workout. The more undercoat you can brush and rake out, the less hair you will have to deal with around the house.

Brushing the Smooth Collie

Using the rubber curry, massage the hair all over his body. Move the curry in a circular motion, and loose hair will come to the surface. Spray coat conditioner or water on his coat. This keeps the outer guard hairs from breaking and helps keep his coat shiny and healthy. Use the pin brush to brush his entire body; then brush him again against the direction the hair grows. This will take out a lot of undercoat. One more brushing in the right direction will clean up all the loose hair. Be sure to brush the extra-furry areas between his legs, under his front legs close to his body, and on his tail.

For a more thorough grooming, especially during shedding season, you may want to use a shedding tool or a shedding blade. After you have brushed him, start with the shedding tool at the rear of the dog. Push some hair in the wrong direction with one hand, and use the shedding tool with your other hand to pull out the undercoat. Let some outer hair drop into place and brush again all the way up the dog's body.

Brushing the Rough Collie

Roughs have long hair all over, even on their legs and feet. Start by misting a section of the coat with water or coat conditioner and then brush, which—like the Smooths—prevents the outer guard hairs from breaking and tames dry hair.

This technique is called "line brushing" because you work one layer of hair at a time, parting the coat as you go. Start at a rear leg, lift a section of hair with your hand and forearm, and brush down and away from it with the pin brush. Next, go over the same spot with the slicker brush to remove the smaller tangles and mats. Then move on to the next section, parting the hair just an inch or so (2.5 cm) above the last line. Work your way up the dog's body toward his head.

Don't neglect his tummy or between his legs. Mats form in the armpitsand under the rear legs, too. You might want to trim a bit under his tail and on his bottom so that he won't get feces stuck in the long hair in this area. Leave the outer hair on his rear "pants" long, and no one will see that his rear end has been cut shorter. In hot weather, you can shave his tummy and no one will be able to tell because the hair at his sides will still be long.

Brush his neck and chest the same way you did for the rest of his body—in layers starting at the bottom and working up. The undercoat is particularly downy and soft here and may need some extra attention. An undercoat rake works especially well in this area to remove loose hair.

Comb his head with a medium- or fine-toothed comb. You'll be amazed by how much the short hair sheds. Comb carefully around his ears, because the long hairs mat easily. Don't cut the mats out; you might cut his ear, especially if he moves suddenly.

As soon as you quit brushing, your Collie will shake himself and his coat should fall into place.

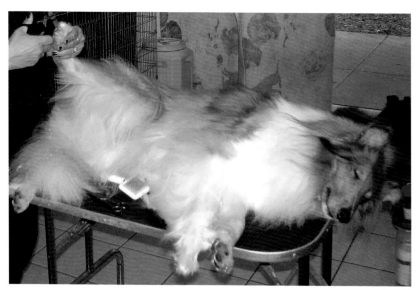

Trim around the outside edge of your Collie's foot to make it look neat.

Trimming Legs, Tummy, and Feet

Owners who show their Collies trim off the long hair on the back of their legs up to the hock in back and to the elbows in front. You can use scissors or clippers. You can also scissor-trim the long, wavy hair hanging down from his tummy for a practical reason—your Collie's coat will pick up grass, burrs, and other bits of outdoor plants and trash. By trimming his coat up off the ground, he'll track less mess into your house.

Hair grows long on a Rough Collie's feet and between his toes. Trim around the outside edge of his foot to make it look neat. On the bottom of his foot, trim hair so that it is even with the bottom of the paw pad. If you have blunt-nosed scissors, you can trim between the pads. While you're grooming his feet, examine them for foxtails, cuts, or other problems.

Foxtails

In late spring, foxtails appear mainly in the western United States. These grass seeds break off into thousands of little stickers and quickly work their way into your dog's coat, between his toes, and in his ears, eyes, or mouth. Foxtails can migrate into the dog's bloodstream and cause serious infection. Sometimes the result can be fatal. Every time your Collie comes inside, check him thoroughly all over, especially along his belly if he's been in tall grass.

GROOMING YOUR COLLIE

Mats

Mats can form anywhere, but most often you'll find them behind your Collie's ears, under his armpits, between his legs, and on his pants in the rear. A neglected Collie will have mats all over his body, chest, and tail. If your dog is sensitive, he won't like you tugging on his coat to get the mats out. Instead, spray the mat with plenty of coat conditioner to make it easier to comb. Hold the mat at its base and brush or comb the ends gently, working down to the skin. You may need to separate the mat with your fingers or brush around the outside edges.

Some mats are too tight to brush out, but don't use scissors. The mat often is so close to your Collie's skin that you'll cut him. Either shave the mats out or take him to a groomer.

BATHING

Collies are naturally very clean. It's easy to brush dirt off the surface of either coat type. You won't have to bathe him often if you keep up with brushing. A Collie's double coat is extremely efficient at keeping his skin dry even in the worst weather. Whether his coat is smooth or rough, the hardest part of a bath is getting your Collie wet down to the skin. You, on the other hand, will probably be soaked!

HOW TO BATHE YOUR COLLIE

Always brush your Collie thoroughly before you bathe him. Wet mats are harder to get out and they don't dry, which causes skin problems such as hot spots.

Bathe your dog in the bathtub or outdoors. Put cotton balls in each of his ears. Use cool or warm water, because hot water irritates dry skin and causes itching. Start with his feet and legs, and using a handheld sprayer, push the water deep into the coat. If you rinse across the top of the coat, the water won't penetrate. Wet his entire body except his head, including his neck and chest. Once he gets water on his face he'll want to shake, so wash his head when you are done with the rest of the body.

Dilute some dog shampoo and apply it in several places on his coat. Scrub it into his entire body with your hands or the pin brush. You can add coat conditioner before or after you rinse, or not at all. (As an alternative, plain white vinegar adds shine to a Smooth Collie's coat.) Now it's time to rinse, rinse, and rinse some more, even for Smoothies. Once again, push the water deep into the coat, all the way to his skin. Start at the front of the dog and work your way back. Rinse until the water runs clear, with no bubbles at all. Any soap residue left on your Collie's skin can cause irritation and hot spots. If you add conditioner after rinsing out the shampoo, repeat the rinsing process. When you're finished, I guarantee he will shake.

Now wash his head. Wet his head carefully, avoiding his ears. Put some diluted shampoo in the palm of your hand or on a washcloth and massage it in. Then thoroughly rinse like you did the body. Hold your Collie's head up and tilt it backward, and try to avoid getting water in his ears. To rinse his muzzle, hold his head level and rinse from the front of his eyes toward his nose. Remember to take the cotton balls out of his ears when you're done.

Towel-dry your Collie thoroughly, and be sure to dry his underside. You can use a hair dryer at a low setting to blow out loose hair and finish drying. Many Collie owners buy professional dryers for their dogs. Caution: Don't use a hot setting on any kind of dryer; it can burn your dog's skin. When he's turned loose, he will run around the house wiping his body against walls and furniture, so you may want to put him in his crate until he's completely dry. Also, don't leave him in a crate with the dryer blowing on him. He can't get away if it gets too hot.

NAIL CARE

As part of your grooming routine, your Collie needs regular nail care. Exercise isn't enough to wear down the nails sufficiently. If his nails grow too long, his feet will splay out, which will affect his ability to walk comfortably. Long toenails also snag on fabric or carpet and scratch your wood floors. Plan to clip his nails weekly while you groom him.

If you introduce the process properly, your Collie won't mind having his nails trimmed. Accompany each session with lots of massage and treats; he'll look forward to it. Run your hand down his leg and hold his paw for a moment, feeding him a treat while you are still holding it. Gradually work up to where you can handle his feet and feel between his toes with ease while feeding him treats. When he is thoroughly used to having his feet handled, introduce the toenail

PUPPY POINTER

Start teaching your puppy to enjoy grooming as soon as you bring him home. When he's ready to settle down after a play session, get down on the floor and lay him between your legs for a massage session. Let him fall asleep for a little bit if he wants. Run your fingers through his coat, massage between his toes, turn him over, and rub his tummy gently. Stick your fingers in his mouth to massage his gums, and stroke his ears and tail. Your puppy will learn to enjoy being handled and groomed, and you'll build a strong bond with each other.

clippers. Have them lying nearby while you handle and brush him so that he gets used to seeing them. Open and shut them to get him acclimated to the sound. Tap his toenail and give him a treat.

HOW TO TRIM YOUR COLLIE'S TOENAILS

Each toenail has a vein of blood down the middle called the "quick," which can be painful and bleed if you accidentally nick it. The quick is easy to see in white nails, but in black toenails, it's impossible. For this reason, trim just the tiniest bit off the end of each nail, less than 1/32 of an inch (.08 cm). Hold the clippers perpendicular to his foot. As you trim each week, the quick will recede and you'll be able to shorten the nails more. The ideal length is even with the end of the foot. At the beginning, give your Collie a treat after each nail is trimmed. Keep sessions short, trimming maybe one foot at a time while he is learning to accept the process.

If you accidentally cut the quick, hold your finger over the end of the nail to stop the bleeding. If you have styptic powder, dab some on the end of the nail to help the blood coagulate. Baking powder or cornstarch may help stem the bleeding if you don't have styptic powder. You'll have a hard time convincing your Collie to let you cut his nails again anytime soon, so start over with the training process.

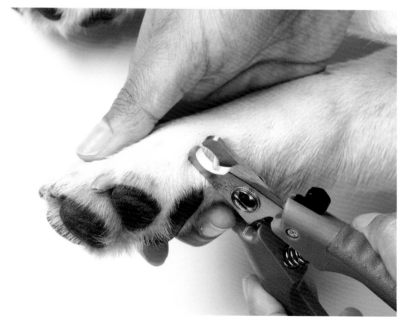

Clipping your Collie's nails is an important part of his grooming routine.

USING A GRINDER TO TRIM TOENAILS

Rotary grinders have a sandpaper cylinder that files down the nail end. You are less likely to hurt the quick with this method because you can quit before you go too far. You can also file off rough edges left by toenail clippers with the grinder. When using a grinder, brush your Collie's leg hair out of the way. Long fur tangles easily in the tool.

Slowly introduce your Collie to the grinder the same way you did with the clippers. Let him hear the noise and give him a treat. Let him feel the vibration of the tool when it's running. Then use it for just a second on the end of the nail. Don't ever grind a nail for more than two or three seconds, because the grinder gets hot and the burning sensation will make him snatch away his foot.

EAR CARE

The upright base of the ear allows air to circulate, so Collies aren't as prone to ear problems as retrievers or hounds are. Keep them dry and wipe them out weekly with a damp gauze pad to remove dirt and prevent infection. Start at the base of the ear and sweep upward with the gauze so that you don't push any bacteria back into the ear. Check for foreign objects, especially foxtails. Never put a cotton swab into the ear; you could puncture the eardrum.

If your Collie's ears have black or bloody-looking gunk in them, or if they smell bad, he may have ear mites or a yeast infection. Both problems cause a dog to shake his head and scratch at his ears. Take your Collie to the vet for medication (ear drops). When you apply the drops, massage the base of the ear to push the liquid deep into the ear canal. He'll shake his head as soon as you're done, which will help coat the ear with medication.

EYE CARE

Collies don't require special care for their eyes, but you should check them if your dog's eyes are red or runny, if he is blinking a lot, or if he's holding his eye partly closed. Examine each eye for grass or other debris. Wipe the eye with a wet gauze pad or cloth, and clean the surrounding area.

If you don't see anything in the eye and the problem persists, take him to the vet. He may have scratched the eye surface itself and will need medicated drops to treat it.

DENTAL CARE

Like all dogs, Collies need regular dental care. By three years old, most dogs have tartar buildup that requires professional teeth cleaning by your vet. Because Collies have such a long muzzle, food often gets caught in the back of the mouth between the teeth and cheek. The food decays and causes bad breath, tartar buildup, and gum disease. You can clean the excess food out with your finger daily, but his teeth still need regular brushing. Brush at least once a week during his regular grooming session.

Excess tartar builds up on the teeth and along the gum line and causes inflammation, which is known as gingivitis. As gum disease progresses, it causes the gums to recede, which creates pockets where food and bacteria become lodged and cause further decay. If dental care is neglected, an infection can develop, spread through the dog's body, and cause organ failure. Gum disease is most common in older dogs.

Dry food and chew toys aren't enough to prevent dental disease. By brushing your Collie's teeth, you will avoid expensive dental bills. When his teeth do need professional cleaning, it won't take as long or be as hard on him.

HOW TO BRUSH YOUR COLLIE'S TEETH

1. Before you use a toothbrush, familiarize your Collie with letting you rub his gums with your fingertips. Besides getting him used to having his mouth handled, this is a relaxation technique used by some massage therapists. When you're ready to actually brush his teeth, use a canine toothbrush, fingertip brush, or even a piece of gauze wrapped around your finger.

Dog Tale

Julie Sandoval is a professional groomer who also shows her Rough and Smooth Collies in conformation and agility. When asked if an owner should ever shave a Rough Collie, she answered: "There is no hard-and-fast rule. Your dog's comfort is the most important thing. That being said, shaving can change the coat's texture, or even the color, when it grows back in. I've seen coats grow back softer, harsher, with patchy color spots, and an assortment of other changes. And sometimes the coat grows in fine and doesn't change at all.

When a dog, especially an older dog, is heavily matted, it may be kinder to shave his coat. If you think you want to shave your Collie because of the heat, try shaving his belly first and see if that is enough. The rough coat provides excellent insulation and takes a long time to grow back in fully. If you live in a really hot climate, thoroughly brushing out the undercoat is usually enough to keep him cool."

2. Add some meat-flavored doggy toothpaste to the brush. Lift his lips and rub over the teeth and gums in small circles with the brush at a slight angle.
3. Open his mouth and brush the molars in the back, paying special attention to the outside of the teeth, which is where food collects.
4. Brush the inside (backs) of his teeth. This area won't have as much buildup because the tongue naturally brushes it.
5. Keep brushing sessions short. If you can't brush your Collie's entire mouth in one sitting, break it up into five-minute sessions until he gets used to it.

GOING TO THE GROOMER

Most Collies need to be professionally groomed occasionally. If you keep up with brushing, he should only need three or four trips a year. A professional groomer has heavy-duty sprayers that can get water through his coat to the skin, and hair dryers that can blow out trashcans full of loose hair.

CHOOSING A GROOMER

Find someone who has experience with double-coated dogs like Shelties and Collies. Ask her if she has groomed Collies and what a full grooming includes versus just a bath and brush out. A full grooming usually includes trimming the feet, legs, and ears, a sanitary cut around the rear, and a toenail trim.

Get your Collie puppy used to brushing his teeth at a young age so that it becomes a normal routine.

HEALTH OF YOUR COLLIE

A Collie who is well cared for can live a long and healthy life. In this chapter we'll help you get started on the right foot with tips on how to protect your Collie from contagious diseases and parasites, and how to recognize the hereditary ailments that affect some Collies. You'll also learn about spaying or neutering your dog and tips for caring for a senior Collie.

FINDING A VETERINARIAN

One of the first things you'll need to do when you bring home your new Collie is schedule a vet exam to ensure he is in good health. When choosing a veterinarian, try to find one who has some experience with Collies and their known health issues.

If your dog's breeder is local, she may be able to refer you to a good veterinarian. Collect recommendations from other dog owners, dog trainers, kennels, and pet sitters. You can also search the member registry at the American Animal Hospital Association website (www.aaha.org).

A vet's bedside manner should be important to you, the pet owner. When you interview a vet, ask her questions and make observations. Does she take time to answer your questions? What are her areas of specialty? Is the staff friendly and helpful? Is the clinic clean and well maintained? If there is more than one vet in the practice, will you be able to choose which vet sees your Collie?

Ask your new veterinarian to recommend a nearby pet emergency hospital that her practice works with. When you are under stress during an emergency, you'll be glad you're prepared.

PUPPY POINTER

Although socialization is important for a puppy's development, don't take him out in public until he finishes his puppy immunizations at 16 weeks old. He can be exposed to diseases like parvovirus just from walking on soil or grass, and is not fully protected until he has had a shot and two boosters.

Carry your puppy to and from the car when you take him somewhere, even to the vet's office. Don't expose him to dogs with unknown vaccine histories, and don't take him to the dog park. Puppy classes require that all puppies be vaccinated, so this is a good place to socialize him. Invite people to your house to meet your Collie pup. Have them remove their shoes before they come in and wash their hands before handling your puppy.

ANNUAL VET VISIT

Your Collie should have an annual checkup even when he isn't due for vaccines. A regular vet exam establishes a baseline "normal" for your dog that the vet can compare to if your dog is ill and as he ages. Your vet will draw blood for your dog's annual heartworm test. She will check your Collie's heart, eyes, ears, weight, and overall body condition. She'll feel for any abnormalities in the organs or limbs. She'll renew and update any prescription medications your dog is taking. She'll answer your questions and recommend any follow-up procedures that might be needed.

CORE VACCINATIONS

When a newborn puppy nurses, his mother's milk provides antibodies that protect him from disease. Once he's weaned off of the milk, the antibodies no longer protect him and he needs a series of vaccines to build his own immunities.

The "core" vaccines that every dog should have prevent distemper, canine hepatitis (also called adenovirus), and parvovirus. These vaccines are administered at 8 weeks, 12 weeks, and 16 weeks. Your puppy isn't fully protected until he has had the full series. A booster is required one year after the last injection.

At 16 weeks, your veterinarian will also administer your puppy's first rabies shot, which is required by law in all 50 states. He will also need a rabies booster in one year. Not coincidentally, 16 weeks is the age at which most jurisdictions require you to license your dog and provide proof of rabies inoculation.

After the one-year vaccines, boosters are recommended every three years. This is a relatively new change in thinking. Previously, animals were revaccinated yearly, but research has shown that most dogs retain enough antibodies to protect them for much longer than a year. Your veterinarian can run a titer, which is a test that shows the presence of the necessary antibodies in your dog's system. The results will help you and your vet decide when your dog needs booster shots.

DISTEMPER

Distemper is a viral infection with symptoms including runny nose, fever, vomiting, and diarrhea. It can also cause neurological problems or bleeding in the intestinal tract, which is quickly fatal.

HEPATITIS

Canine hepatitis is caused by an adenovirus (CAV-1) and is often transmitted to dogs by foxes or coyotes. An infected dog will have a fever and enlarged lymph nodes. Internal hemorrhaging, liver disease, and swelling in the brain rapidly cause death.

PARVOVIRUS

Parvovirus is extremely contagious and stays in the environment for up to five months, so protection by vaccine is very important. Symptoms include bloody diarrhea, fever, and depression. There is no cure, but it is treated with fluids and medication to control the symptoms. Few dogs survive the disease.

RABIES

Rabies is an ancient and deadly disease caused by a virus; it's commonly transmitted to dogs from infected wild animals, including skunks, bats, and foxes. An infected dog will become increasingly aggressive and nervous, which advances to paralysis. It is always fatal.

NONCORE VACCINATIONS

Additional vaccines are available but not required. Noncore vaccines include those for bordetella (kennel cough), coronavirus, leptospirosis, Lyme disease, parainfluenza, and rattlesnake venom. Whether or not your dog needs them depends on where you are located and the incidence of the diseases in your area.

If you live in a wooded area or go hiking with your dog, consider getting him vaccinated for Lyme disease.

Because you don't want to overload your dog's system by giving him too many vaccines at once, discuss the options with your vet before you make a decision.

BORDETELLA

Also called kennel cough, bordetella comprises a group of upper-respiratory illnesses that cause a dry, hacking cough. Bordetella is highly contagious and spreads through the air when a dog coughs or sneezes. Similar to the common cold in humans, it lasts about a week. If the coughing is severe, your vet may suggest a cough suppressant; otherwise, no treatment is required. Kennel cough can develop into something more serious, like pneumonia.

Kennels and dog day care facilities require a bordetella vaccine every six months. The vaccine doesn't prevent all strains of kennel cough, but it provides some protection.

CORONAVIRUS

Coronavirus used to be considered one of the core vaccines, but the disease is not usually fatal and responds well to treatment, so the vaccine is rarely recommended. The main symptoms are diarrhea and severe dehydration.

LEPTOSPIROSIS

If there are known cases of leptospirosis in your area, consider giving your dog the vaccine. This is a bacterial disease transmitted primarily by mice and rats. It

Dog Tale

I took my Collie, Emma, to rattlesnake avoidance training along with my Lab, Tank. The two reacted very differently to the live snakes. At the end of the training, I had to call my dog to come to me while a snake (with his mouth taped shut) was in his path. Tank gave the snake a wide berth and then hurried to my side. Emma, on the other hand, stood completely still and wouldn't move a muscle. Throughout the training, she would barely move or would quietly avoid the snake rather than alert me to its presence. She didn't show any fear and was much more thoughtful than the other dogs. Typical for a Collie, you could see her trying to figure out the situation.

can also contaminate rivers and streams. It is a "zoonotic" disease, meaning it is transmissible from animals to humans.

LYME DISEASE

Lyme disease is one of several tick-borne diseases and is contracted when an infected tick bites your dog. Consider vaccinating your Collie if you spend a lot of time hiking in the woods or if ticks are common in your area.

PARAINFLUENZA

Parainfluenza is a more serious and contagious virus in the kennel cough family, and it spreads quickly among groups of dogs. Symptoms include coughing, runny nose, and fever. This disease can lead to secondary pneumonia and death.

RATTLESNAKE VENOM

This vaccine protects against Western diamondback rattlesnake venom and provides some protection against the Eastern diamondback venom. If your dog is bitten by either snake, even after being vaccinated, he'll still need to see a vet right away. Also consider rattlesnake avoidance training for your Collie.

PARASITES

Dogs are subject to infestation by both internal and external parasites, all of which are treatable. Your Collie is more likely to be affected by parasites depending on the time of year and where you take him hiking in the woods.

EXTERNAL PARASITES

Fleas

You'll know your Collie has fleas if you see flea dirt—little white and black specks—on his skin. The white specks are flea eggs and the black specks are droppings, which turn blood red when wet. In a severe case, when you inspect his tummy, you'll see fleas running for cover. Fleas congregate in warm places: the underbelly, ears, and armpits. Besides treating your dog, you'll need to treat your house, yard, furniture, and bedding to completely eliminate the fleas.

Prevent a flea infestation on your dog by applying a monthly preventive treatment, either topical or oral. A topical treatment is applied between your dog's shoulder blades, where it is distributed into the oil glands of the skin. It kills the fleas within several hours. Monthly oral preventive treatments are also available and many preventive flea treatments protect against ticks.

Ticks

Ticks carry diseases that are dangerous to people and dogs, such as Lyme disease, Rocky Mountain spotted fever, and erhlichiosis. Collies and people pick up ticks while walking through tall grass or hiking in the woods. The tick burrows into the skin and drinks the dog's blood, injecting disease-causing bacteria at the same time. Go over your Collie's body thoroughly after hiking. Ticks are smaller than

Check your Collie for fleas and ticks after he's been outside.

a pencil point and are easy to remove before they attach to the skin. Once attached, they are hard to kill; you can't just crush them with your fingers.

When a tick is attached and filled with blood, it looks like a grape hanging off of your dog. Use tweezers or a tick puller, and grasp the tick firmly at the skin. You must remove the tick's head, which is buried in the skin. Pull slowly to extract the entire tick. Douse the tick in alcohol or insecticide. Once you've removed it, clean your dog's skin and apply some antibiotic ointment to prevent infection. If your Collie's skin remains irritated and red, see your veterinarian.

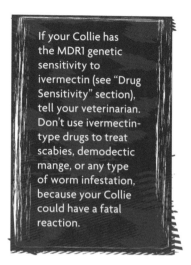

If your Collie has the MDR1 genetic sensitivity to ivermectin (see "Drug Sensitivity" section), tell your veterinarian. Don't use ivermectin-type drugs to treat scabies, demodectic mange, or any type of worm infestation, because your Collie could have a fatal reaction.

Demodectic Mange

Demodectic mange (demodicosis or demodex) is a mite that's present on all dogs, but it usually doesn't cause a problem unless your dog has a compromised immune system due to stress or illness. Symptoms of demodex are scaly reddened skin on the face or forelegs, hair loss, pustules, and plugged hair follicles. If demodex becomes generalized (spreads all over the body), secondary skin infections can develop. A vet can diagnose the mites by examining a skin scraping. Miticidal dips are the prescribed treatment, and antibiotics are prescribed to treat skin infection.

Ear Mites

A dog infested with ear mites (otodectes cynotis) will have a reddish-brown, waxy buildup in his ears. He'll shake his head, scratch his ears, and probably won't want you to touch them. Ear mites can also lead to yeast or bacterial infections. Once your veterinarian diagnoses your dog with ear mites, he will need a miticide and a prescription antibiotic or anti-inflammatory ointment to cure any resulting infections.

Ringworm

Ringworm is a fungal infection that was very common decades ago, and still occurs occasionally. These fungi invade the skin, hair, and nails and cause itching and hair loss, leaving scaly bald patches on your dog's skin. Oral and topical medications are used to treat the condition. It is highly contagious to other animals and people through direct contact with an infected animal, or via shed skin cells and hair.

Sarcoptic Mange

Also called scabies, sarcoptic mange (sarcoptes scabiei) consists of mites that burrow into your dog's skin, cause intense itching, and are highly contagious. Besides constant itching, your dog will lose hair on his elbows and on the edges of his ears, face, and tummy. Scabies are hard to see under a microscope, so the diagnosis is often assumed based on the symptoms. Treatment includes miticidal dips, shampoos, and anti-inflammatory medication.

INTERNAL PARASITES

When treating your dog for any type of worms, be careful not to use products that contain ivermectin, unless your Collie is clear of the MDR1 gene sensitivity to this drug. You can read more about this inherited problem in Collies in the following "Breed-Specific Illnesses" section.

An annual heartworm test and monthly preventive protects your dog from the disease.

Heartworms

An infected mosquito injects heartworm microfilaria into the bloodstream when it bites your Collie. The microfilaria mature and travel through the body to the pulmonary arteries of the heart, where they reproduce. Adult heartworms cause an enlarged heart and high blood pressure. Heartworm ultimately causes congestive heart failure and organ damage. Treatment involves intravenous arsenic injections. At the same time, your dog must rest completely, which usually requires crate confinement. The treatment takes several months and is hard on a dog.

Heartworm is easy to prevent—an annual heartworm test and a monthly preventive treatment will protect your dog.

Hookworms, Roundworms, and Whipworms

Hookworms, roundworms, and whipworms are three common intestinal parasites that can infect dogs of all ages. Dogs pick up the worms from contaminated soil and feces. A veterinarian can find them during a microscopic examination of a stool sample. An infected dog has a dull, dry coat, weight loss, diarrhea, vomiting, or anemia. Puppies will have a rounded, swollen tummy. It takes at least two treatments, about two weeks apart, to get all the worms out of your dog's system. The first treatment kills the live worms, and the second dose kills those that have hatched and developed since the first dose.

Most puppies have worms, which are usually passed from the mother to her puppies; it doesn't mean the breeder did anything wrong. Most puppies are dewormed at least once before going to their new homes.

Tapeworms

Fleas can cause tapeworms, which are entirely different from other intestinal worms. They look like grains of rice and appear around your dog's rectum or in his stool. Your dog may also scoot his rear end on the floor. When your dog bites at fleas he ingests the eggs, which hatch into tapeworms and grow in his intestinal tract. Your vet will prescribe a medication to kill the tapeworms, which is different from the medication that kills other types of worms. Vigilant flea prevention will keep your dog from being reinfected.

SPAY OR NEUTER YOUR COLLIE

All pet dogs should be spayed or neutered (altered). Hundreds of thousands of dogs, including Collies, are euthanized in shelters every year. Check with any Collie rescue group and you'll find they always have a number of homeless dogs waiting to be adopted.

Altered dogs are easier to live with. A female in heat is messy because you have to take care of the bloody discharge. An unaltered female will also attract unneutered males from miles around, and she'll be crabby and irritable, especially toward other female dogs. Both unaltered males and females will try to escape to breed, so they are difficult to confine. Intact males are more likely to challenge each other and fight. Neutered males may still urine mark, but not nearly as often.

Talk to your veterinarian about when to alter your Collie. Recent research suggests that sex hormones play a big part in bone growth and development, so

it is better to wait until your dog is 12 to 18 months old. But at the same time, you don't want an accidental litter, and a very young mother isn't physically or mentally ready to care for puppies.

BREED-SPECIFIC ILLNESSES

BLOAT

Large, deep-chested dogs—including Collies—are at risk for bloat, also known as gastric dilation volvulus (GDV). When GDV occurs, it is a life-threatening emergency. The stomach fills with excess gas and fluid, and may twist. GDV sometimes strikes older dogs who are in poor health. Symptoms develop suddenly and include obvious discomfort, salivating, trying to vomit, and an enlarged abdomen.

If not treated quickly with emergency surgery, a dog can go into shock and die. The surgeon repositions the stomach and may tack it to the intestinal wall. Up to 50 percent of dogs with bloat die, and survivors are likely to have a recurrence.

Researchers feel that bloat has any number of causes, and sometimes there is no obvious reason at all. One suspected cause is that a dog who eats or

HEALTH OF YOUR COLLIE

81

drinks large amounts quickly will gulp excess air, which fills up the stomach. To prevent bloat:

• Feed your Collie at least twice a day.
• Soak your dog's food so it will expand in his bowl, not in his stomach.
• Be sure that your Collie doesn't exercise vigorously one hour before and after meals.

COLLIE EYE ANOMALY (CEA)

An inherited eye disease, Collie eye anomaly (CEA) exists in almost 70 percent of Collies and consists of two major structural abnormalities of the eye: choroidal hypoplasia and colobomas. The milder abnormality, choroidal hypoplasia is a deficiency of the blood vessels located immediately behind the retina at the very back of the eyeball. Collies with choroidal hypoplasia alone generally suffer no adverse effects throughout their lives, since the condition does not usually progress. Other Collies with CEA are born with outpouchings, or "pits," in the eye tissue layers near the optic nerve called colobomas, which are a more severe form of CEA. These colobomas represent a severely weakened and irregular area of tissue that can progress to retinal detachment and blindness even at a young age. CEA can affect one or both eyes, so even dogs with the most severe form may not suffer complete blindness. There is no treatment or cure for CEA.

COLLIE

A veterinary ophthalmologist examines a puppy's eyes at five to eight weeks old to detect CEA, and dogs are diagnosed as either "clear" or "affected" based on their appearance. A genetic (blood) test for CEA is available.

COLLIE PRA

The type of progressive retinal atrophy (PRA) found in Collies is also called rod-cone dysplasia type 2 (rcd2). This is when the rods and cones in the eye (light-sensitive cells) develop abnormally and cause night blindness, which progresses to total blindness. A genetic test is available for this type of PRA, and dogs are identified as clear, carriers, or affected. PRA is much easier to eliminate than CEA in Collies, and affected dogs should not be bred.

DERMATOMYOSITIS (DM)

Dermatomyositis (DM) is an inherited inflammatory disorder that first affects the skin, causing lesions and inflammation, and later causes muscle wasting in affected Collies. Symptoms can appear in dogs as young as six months of age and include hair loss, blisters, bumps, and crusting on the skin. The muzzle, ear tips, tip of the tail, toes, and elbows are most often affected. In some dogs, symptoms flare up and recede, and sometimes seem to disappear.

The muscles in the face, head, and legs may atrophy in Collies who develop muscular symptoms. A severely affected dog may have trouble chewing or swallowing. Other dogs may have such mild muscle symptoms that the owner doesn't notice them. A veterinarian will confirm the diagnosis by taking a skin biopsy and having it analyzed. DM is aggravated by sunlight, so owners should apply sunscreen on an affected Collie's skin. Vets may prescribe steroids for occasional flare-ups of the condition. Vitamin E can help prevent scarring.

DISCOID LUPUS ERYTHEMATOSUS

Also known as "Collie nose," discoid lupus erythematosus (DLE) is an inflammatory skin disease. The first symptom is usually loss of pigment on the dog's nose. Instead of black, his nose turns a patchy pink. DLE may also affect the lips, around the eyes, and the bridge of the nose, but doesn't affect other areas of the body. The condition is managed with sunscreens, vitamin E, and occasional treatment with oral medications.

DRUG SENSITIVITY

Collies and some other white-footed herding breeds are affected by a mutation in the MDR1 gene. The MDR1 gene mutation is a defect in a protein that enables

the brain to transport drugs out of the brain and into the blood. It is estimated that as many as 70 percent of Collies are affected by this abnormality. Some commonly used drugs that can cause toxicity and even death in Collies with this mutation include ivermectin (deworming medication), acepromazine (tranquilizer), and Imodium (antidiarrheal medication). Other drugs can also cause severe and even fatal reactions. An affected dog will have seizures, severe neurological symptoms, and may die.

A genetic test is now available for the MDR1 gene, so you can find out if your Collie should avoid these drugs. A dog with any form of the mutation is at risk for severe neurological symptoms, even when a drug is administered at low doses.

HIP AND ELBOW DYSPLASIA

Collies are not as prone to inherited hip or elbow dysplasia as other large breeds, but it does occur occasionally. Hip dysplasia develops when the ball of the femur doesn't fit properly into the hip socket. Elbow dysplasia is caused by abnormal development of the bones in the elbow joints. Both conditions cause arthritis and lameness due to joint pain.

Dogs with dysplasia can be mildly affected and never show symptoms, or they can be severely affected and require surgery to correct the condition or replace the joints. Treatments include anti-inflammatory drugs and mild, non-weight-bearing exercises, such as walking and swimming.

Most Collie breeders have their dogs' hips and elbows x-rayed at two years old, when their joints are fully formed. The images are sent to the Orthopedic Foundation for Animals, where hip x-rays are graded from excellent (the best) to severe (the worst). Elbows are not graded if they are normal, but abnormal x-rays are rated Grade I (mild) to Grade III (severe degenerative disease). Affected dogs should not be bred.

SEIZURES

Collies can inherit epilepsy or other seizure disorders. If your dog has a seizure, take him to the vet immediately. Some seizures stop in a few seconds or minutes, but others continue until the doctor can administer anticonvulsant medication or tranquilizers. A complete vet exam and blood work may uncover an underlying health problem that caused the seizures, or they could be "idiopathic"—of an unknown cause. A vet may prescribe regular doses of phenobarbital or another anticonvulsant medication for a dog who has frequent seizures.

THYROID DISORDERS

Hypothyroidism affects some Collies and occurs when the thyroid doesn't produce enough of the thyroid hormone. It usually begins between four

If your Collie seems more sluggish than usual, take him to the vet to check him for hyperthyroidism or other health issues.

to ten years of age and has a variety of symptoms, so owners often don't recognize it at first. Dogs with hypothyroidism are sometimes overweight, sluggish, intolerant of exercise or cold weather, and suffer from hair loss, greasy skin, and infections. It's not until 70 percent of the thyroid gland is damaged that symptoms become recognizable.

A blood test is used to diagnose thyroid problems. Treatment consists of a twice-daily dose of a synthetic thyroid hormone for the rest of the dog's life.

VON WILLEBRAND DISEASE (VWD)

An inherited bleeding disorder that affects Collies, von Willebrand disease (vWD) is a deficiency in blood clotting ability, similar to hemophilia in humans. It causes excessive bleeding and bruising in affected dogs. Some dogs aren't diagnosed until they have surgery and develop pockets of blood at the incision site. Genetic testing is available to identify Collies as clear, a carrier, or affected. Affected dogs should not be bred. There is no cure, but once you know your dog is affected, your veterinarian can take precautions during medical procedures.

GENERAL ILLNESSES

ALLERGIES

The most common allergies in dogs are flea allergic dermatitis, environmental allergies, and food allergies. Flea saliva can cause an itchy reaction even if there is only one flea on your dog. Diligent flea prevention is the best treatment. Secondary infections from irritated skin are common and treated with antibiotics.

Environmental allergies include sensitivity to grass, pollen, dust mites, and other irritants that are impossible to eliminate from your surroundings. This

Dog Tale

Gayle Kaye, of Chelsea Collies in Valley Center, California, is a board member of the Collie Health Foundation, an American Kennel Club (AKC)-licensed judge for Collies, and the author of two books about the history of the breed. She was asked if Collies were ever in the top ten AKC breeds and if their popularity hurt the breed in any way.

According to Gayle, "Collies were the most-registered AKC breed in 1905 and 1910, and repeatedly in the top ten up into the 1970s. First there was the popularity of Lad in the early years. Then with the release of *Lassie Come Home* in the 40s, there was another surge, and their numbers continued to increase with Lassie's popularity in the 1950s and 60s. Whenever a breed is so popular, irresponsible people think they are going to make a lot of money selling dogs. Collie health problems became more prevalent because breeders didn't carefully choose healthy dogs to breed. That may have contributed to Collie popularity dropping off a bit over the years. One thing I have seen is that Collie owners are very loyal to the breed and come back time and again over the decades to get another Collie."

is often a seasonal problem. Sometimes soaking your dog's feet removes allergens that he tracks in from outdoors. Air purifiers and other measures similar to those taken by people with allergic reactions can also help your Collie. Benadryl (diphenhydramine), an antihistamine, doesn't make dogs sleepy like it does people, and dogs can take it safely. Ask your veterinarian to calculate the proper dose for your Collie's weight.

DIARRHEA

Overly soft or runny stools can be a one-time problem or may indicate a serious illness. If there is blood or mucus in the stool, take a sample to your vet for analysis. Also look for worms in the stool. When your Collie is ready to eat again, start out slowly with plain, skinless baked chicken or ground turkey and canned pumpkin. The fiber in the pumpkin will help firm up his stools.

A dog with diarrhea can quickly become dehydrated, so be sure your Collie has plenty of water available. Lethargy or loss of appetite can be symptoms of something more serious. Take him to the vet if the condition lasts more than a day or two.

VOMITING

Occasional vomiting is another symptom that can be a one-time event or an indicator of serious illness. Dogs eat disagreeable things all the time; they are scavengers by nature. Vomiting can sometimes be a good thing. It helps rid the body of things that don't agree with his tummy before they are completely digested or lodged in his stomach. Continuous vomiting is a sign of a problem, and you should take your Collie to the vet if this occurs. Retching without producing anything may be a sign of bloat.

ALTERNATIVE THERAPIES

Some pet owners turn to alternative means of treating their Collies when traditional medicine hasn't been effective. Acupuncture and chiropractic, homeopathic, and herbal therapies are often used alongside conventional Western medicine to treat pain and disease, and relieve conditions such as stress or separation anxiety. These therapies don't work for every dog, but in many cases, they can help your dog's recovery and make him comfortable. Always work with your veterinarian or another expert practitioner so you'll have realistic expectations and ensure that the remedy will not harm your dog.

ACUPUNCTURE

Acupuncture has been practiced for thousands of years and has its roots in Chinese medicine. Practitioners strive to correct energy imbalances in the body by inserting needles along meridians, or energy paths, on the body. Acupuncture is often used to treat pain and inflammation from arthritis, dysplasia, injuries, and neurological or digestive disorders.

CHIROPRACTIC THERAPY

Chiropractic therapy is often recommended for Collies with arthritis, hip or elbow dysplasia, and injuries. Treatment involves manipulating his spine to realign the vertebrae, increase range of motion, and improve the nervous system's functioning. The American Veterinary Medical Association (AVMA) recommends that a vet examine your dog before you pursue chiropractic treatment. Choose a chiropractor who specializes in animals and is a member of the American Veterinary Chiropractic Association (AVCA).

HOMEOPATHY

Homeopathy is the practice of using highly diluted remedies to cure disease. It is based on the concept that "like produces like." Practitioners use a substance that causes a certain symptom in its pure, undiluted form. In its highly diluted form, the same substance relieves that symptom. Some remedies are used to treat a variety of symptoms at once.

Plants and flowers have been used to heal since ancient times.

Don't rely solely on homeopathic remedies to cure your dog. If you are interested in homeopathic remedies, consult with your veterinarian or a homeopathic practitioner. Purchase only well-known, brand-name remedies since there is no government regulation of these substances.

HERBAL REMEDIES

Plants and flowers have been used since ancient times to heal. Herbal remedies can be purchased, or you can make them yourself in the form of teas, dried plants, roots, or tinctures. For example, chamomile is a commonly known herbal remedy that calms the system and relieves digestive distress.

FIRST AID

Learn some simple first-aid techniques so that you can keep calm in an emergency. Consider attending a pet first-aid course so you are prepared if something happens to your dog. Most serious mishaps will need veterinary attention, but there are a few things you can do help him immediately. Some common situations in which you can help include trauma (impact with a car, puncture wound, broken bone), heatstroke, snakebite, or poisoning.

- **Trauma:** Assess the injury and call your vet for further instructions. Stabilize broken bones by making a splint with sticks or a rolled magazine, and wrap the limb with gauze. Don't remove any sticks or other items lodged in the wound because it could make the bleeding worse. Transport your dog to the vet immediately. If you know how, administer animal CPR if it's needed.

- **Heatstroke:** Dogs can suffer from heatstroke much faster than people, so if your Collie is suddenly tired and wants to rest, pay attention. Find some shade and give him some water. Symptoms of heatstroke include panting, drooling, thick saliva, bright red gums, or appearing disoriented. He can quickly go into shock and die. Dogs don't sweat, so cool his paw pads with water and place cool wet towels over his body. Take him to the vet as quickly as possible to prevent damage to his internal organs and for further care.
- **Snakebite:** Try to indentify the type of snake that bit your dog without endangering your own safety. Most bites are to the legs or face, so your Collie's thick fur won't be much protection. Don't suck the venom out! And don't apply a tourniquet; it can do more harm than good. If possible, carry your dog to the car so the venom won't spread too quickly through his system. Take him to the vet immediately. A snakebite is very painful even if the snake doesn't inject any venom. The amount of venom a snake injects can vary wildly and is not affected by the size of the snake, so treat all bites as life-threatening until you know for sure.
- **Poisoning:** A curious dog will ingest snail or rodent bait, chocolate, yard or household chemicals, or other toxic substances. Symptoms include vomiting, trembling, seizure, and heavy drooling. If you can identify the poison, it will help your vet decide what treatment to use. Call the vet immediately; she may instruct you to induce vomiting. If your dog has had time to digest the poison, vomiting won't be sufficient and he'll need further treatment with IV fluids and other supportive care.

FIRST-AID KIT

Keep a first-aid kit handy in case of emergencies. It should include:
- 3-percent hydrogen peroxide for cleaning and disinfecting a wound
- adhesive tape to wrap bandages or splints
- antibiotic ointment to treat minor wounds or bites
- blankets and towels to carry a dog, cover him up if he's in shock, and for cleanup
- cotton batting to make a large bandage or wrap around an injured leg
- diphenhydramine (Benadryl) for allergic reaction to insect bites and stings
- gauze bandages and gauze pads to protect small wounds
- muzzle to prevent an injured or frightened dog from biting
- rectal thermometer to take your dog's temperature
- safety pins for securing bandages
- saline eyewash to flush debris or soothe an injured eye
- blunt-tipped scissors to cut bandages, tape, or something out of your dog's fur
- strips of clean cloth to secure a splint or bandage

- tweezers to remove small debris from between toes or in the ears; also to remove stingers or ticks
- wooden paint-mixing sticks for splints

SENIOR DOGS

Large dogs are considered seniors at eight years old, but your Collie will probably still be active and healthy for several more years. Watch for age-related changes, and be prepared to help him by doing the following:

- He should have a senior wellness exam to establish a baseline of information for the veterinarian to compare to as he ages.
- Arthritis is the main problem Collies face in old age. Your dog may have trouble walking on hard floors or getting in and out of the car. Put down carpet runners to help him get around. A ramp will help him get in and out of the car.
- Anti-inflammatory medications will help him stay comfortable.
- Encourage your Collie to stay as active as possible with daily walks. Exercise alleviates stiffness from old age ailments like arthritis.
- Switch to senior food with higher fiber and fewer calories. Consider adding digestive enzymes to his food to keep his tummy healthy.
- Provide an orthopedic bed made with egg-crate foam to cushion older joints.
- Senior dogs are more susceptible to extreme heat and cold; keep him indoors and out of extreme weather.

In senior dogs, exercise helps alleviate stiffness from arthritis.

TRAINING YOUR COLLIE

We all know deep in our hearts that Lassie would save us if we fell in a well. Collies have quite a reputation to live up to. Fictional Collies Lassie and Lad have convinced the world that all Collies are perfect. When you are out and about with your Collie, you'll often hear people exclaim, "I had a Collie when I was growing up!" as their eyes get misty with the memory of that beloved, perfect dog.

So here you sit with your diamond in the rough, certain that he can be the perfect Collie, too. The good news is Collies have earned their sterling reputation because they are smart, loving, loyal, and trainable. Think of what the Collie was bred to do; he spends long hours herding sheep for his owner in all types of weather. He works at a distance from the shepherd and often solves problems alone.

Collies are eager to learn and easy to teach. They are sensitive to your moods and require a soft touch, but they also need gentle discipline to rope in their enthusiasm. In fact, without training and discipline, your Collie won't grow up to be Lassie at all. He needs you to show him the way. A few months of training is worth it when the result is 13 years or more with a well-behaved Collie.

By incorporating lessons into his everyday life, you'll find that training your dog is fun and useful. You'll use obedience commands throughout the day so he learns to walk nicely at your side, sit while you attach the leash, politely greet people, and rest quietly on his bed while you eat dinner.

Use positive reinforcement to help train your Collie and get the behavior you want.

Collies are eager to learn and easy to teach.

At about the fourth or fifth week of training, your Collie may suddenly forget everything you taught him. This is because it takes Collies at least six weeks of training for a new behavior to become a habit, as it converts from their short-term memory to long-term memory. (That's why many obedience classes are six weeks long.) Keep working with him even if you have to take a few steps back, and this learning plateau will soon pass.

POSITIVE TRAINING METHODS

Your Collie is always learning—even when you aren't actively teaching him something. He doesn't know the difference between right and wrong because he doesn't speak your language. Dogs communicate by reading body language, and Collies are experts at it. Herding dogs are visually oriented; they carefully watch the sheep, anticipating every move. A Collie reacts quickly, almost before the sheep can change direction. His eagle eye is on you, too.

Rewarded behavior will be repeated. Without rewards, he doesn't know when he's doing the right thing. If something wonderful happens every time he sits, he'll be offering a *sit* even when you're not asking for it. By patiently showing him how to do what you want and rewarding him while he's doing it, he'll learn quickly.

Figure out what is rewarding to your Collie. Try high-value treats, meaning something he never gets except in exchange for a correct behavior. A dog who won't work for kibble or biscuits might get enthusiastic over small pieces of cheese, cooked chicken, or hot dog. Try to come up with additional rewards, like a squeaky toy that you can hide in your pocket and pull out when you need it.

Collies are very sensitive and will shut down if trained with harsh corrections. If he thinks he's going to be punished, he'll actively avoid you as soon as he sees the leash. Collies are also thinkers; they're not blindly obedient. Once they've done something right, they see no reason to repeat the exercise and will even consider it punishment when they have to do the same thing over and over. A bored Collie might add his own variations since, in his mind, the last thing he did obviously wasn't quite right.

SOCIALIZATION

Socialization is the process of introducing your Collie to as much of the outside world as possible so that new people and things won't frighten him. Dogs react to something unfamiliar and scary in one of three ways: freezing, fleeing, or fighting. He'll freeze to evaluate the threat, flee if he's frightened, or fight if he can't get away. Dogs who aren't socialized properly at a young age are more likely to choose the third option and bite, or otherwise react aggressively. A well-socialized puppy grows up capable of meeting new challenges without overreacting.

A good breeder will start the socialization process as soon as the puppy opens his eyes. When you bring your Collie puppy home, continue his education. At this age his vision isn't fully matured, so he recognizes shapes more than individuals. That's why your puppy should meet people of all kinds: tall, short, heavy, thin, young, and old. People wearing uniforms or hats, carrying an umbrella, or sitting in a wheelchair are all very different to him.

Another part of his socialization is to introduce your new puppy to hundreds of sights, sounds, smells, and other animals—for example, the vacuum cleaner, dishwasher, bicycle, car, grooming tools, television, cats, horses, and other dogs.

Don't force a puppy to approach something he is not sure of, especially when you first bring him home. The period of 7 to 12 weeks old is called the "fear imprint period," where if something traumatic happens, he may remember and be afraid of it for the rest of his life. A similar fear period reappears at about six to seven months old and lasts a few weeks. He'll act cautious and afraid of things that didn't bother him in the slightest a week ago. Your reaction in most cases should be to act happy, as if nothing is bothering you. He'll take his cue from you. Don't comfort him, or he'll decide there really is something to be afraid of. Be confident and patient. Allow him to get used to the person, animal, or object from a distance at his own speed. He'll gradually become more confident.

If you have just adopted an adult dog, introduce him to the world as if he is an eight-week-old puppy. He'll be receptive to new things because everything is new to him in unfamiliar surroundings. You'll get to know each other and build a bond while he's still looking to you for reassurance.

Socialization is a lifelong process. Once your Collie's vaccines are complete, expand his social circle so he continues to encounter new people, places, and things.

SOCIALIZING WITH CHILDREN

Collies are wonderful family dogs. Teach your Collie how to behave around children and teach the kids how to behave with a dog. Never leave your dog alone with children—you need to supervise and control their interactions. A puppy will quickly get tired, so keep initial introductions short and with just one or two kids. Teach the kids how to pet the puppy, toss a toy a short way, feed him a treat, or brush him. As the pup grows, they can walk him on a leash and have him perform some obedience commands or tricks.

Things get pretty noisy and active with a lot of kids running around screaming, and your Collie needs to get used to this without being overwhelmed. As a herding dog, he'll want to move the kids into a circle all the while nipping at their heels. When the action starts to get wild, put him on a leash and reward him for his self-control. A time out for everyone usually calms things down.

MEETING OTHER DOGS

Puppies should meet other dogs and learn manners from their peers, who won't hurt them. Other puppies will teach your Collie not to bite too hard or play too rough. Until your Collie reaches maturity, adult dogs will recognize that he is a puppy and not a threat, so they will tolerate a lot of puppy nonsense before disciplining him. He needs to learn these lessons, so don't step in unless you sense the adult dog is fed up with his antics.

Collies generally get along well with other dogs. Dogs communicate by sniffing each other. They use body language to say, "I'm not a threat" or "Let's play." They'll dance around with their tails up and ears alert. One dog may try

to mount another and be sharply disciplined, or one may play bow and ask another to chase him. Give them lots of room so they aren't crowded or likely to act defensively. Introduce dogs on neutral territory.

CRATE TRAINING

A dog's den is his castle, and your Collie's den is his crate. Don't think of it as a cage; think of it as your child's bedroom. The "room" is really his own little world where he can rest and enjoy time to himself. The crate is an essential housetraining tool. It's a safe place for him when you have guests or workers at the house. When you travel with your dog, bring the crate so that he has a safe and familiar place to sleep. He'll settle down quickly at the vet or a boarding kennel if he's already accustomed to confinement. A Collie who is happy in his crate gets to be in the house where all the action is, not stuck out in the backyard alone.

Your breeder may have started the crate-training process. Teach puppies and adult dogs the same way. You want him to enjoy spending time in his crate. Toss a few treats just inside the crate. Let him poke his head in and take the treats while you hang back. You don't want him to be afraid that you're going to shove him in there. Do this several times a day, gradually tossing the treats farther back in the crate four or five times. At dinnertime, set his food bowl just inside the crate and leave him alone. Place his next meal a little farther back in the crate. If he is hesitant to step on the crate floor, put in a towel or bedding. Continue with the treat and meal sessions until he's comfortable going in the crate. At some point, close the door and immediately open it again before he has a chance to get upset. Work up to where you're able to shut the door for a minute or more.

Don't let him out until he is quiet. Try to anticipate when he's going to fuss, and let him out before he gets the chance. Leave the door shut for a shorter period next time. Never let him out when he is barking or scratching at the crate door. He'll learn that throwing a tantrum means he gets his way, and he'll be even more persistent next time. Be patient and let him out as soon as he settles down, even for a moment. Gradually build up the time he spends in the crate. Crate training should take about a week.

Practice crate time when you are going to be at home, varying the amount of time he's in his crate. Sit nearby reading or watching television and walk in and out of the room several times. Let him sleep in his crate in your bedroom. Give him a special chew toy that he only gets when he's crated. He'll look forward to it. My own dogs run to their crates and stand in the doorway waiting for me to deliver their treat and shut the door.

You should never leave your Collie in his crate all day while you are at work and then all night while you sleep.

HOUSETRAINING

A young puppy has no control over his bodily functions; when he feels the urge to go, he eliminates wherever he is. An eight-week-old puppy can only hold it for about an hour, so he will need frequent trips outside during the first few weeks. By 10 to 12 weeks old, he should be able to sleep through the night without a potty break. He won't be fully housetrained until about four months of age. Collies are very tidy and housetrain quickly.

Pick a spot in the yard that the entire family agrees on for the puppy's toilet area. He'll recognize the smell and know what he's there for after a few trips outside. At first, take him out once an hour, especially when he wakes up, after he eats, after he drinks, after a nap, after a play session, and before bedtime. You'll learn to recognize the signs that he is getting ready to have an accident. He'll circle and sniff, looking for just the right spot.

Go outside with him every time until he is completely housetrained. If you don't go with him, he won't connect the outing with relieving himself, and you won't know whether he's done his business or not. He'll wait at the back door for you rather than take care of business. Don't play with him; just wait. When he goes, praise him profusely, like he's the smartest Collie you've ever seen. Why, even Lassie isn't that smart! He needs to know that he's pleased you, and this is how he'll know. Now he can go back inside and have some free playtime. If he doesn't go, take him inside, put him in his crate for 15 minutes, and try again.

Once he eliminates and has had some free time, put him in his crate until it's time to go out again. Once he starts to get the idea, put a verbal command with the action, like, "Hurry up," or "Go potty." Follow this strict schedule for several weeks. He'll soon be able to hold it for longer periods.

PUPPY POINTER

Collies are slower to mature than other herding breeds, such as Australian Shepherds. In terms of concentration and attentiveness, what you will see an Aussie do at age 1½, a Collie won't be able to do until he is two. They are just puppies for longer. Owners need to exercise patience when teaching their Collie, especially with self-control exercises like the *stay*. He'll get it; it will just take a while.

Use pet gates to confine your Collie in the room with you so you can catch him in the act or, better yet, prevent an accident. If your puppy has an accident in the house, don't rub his nose in it or spank him with a newspaper. He doesn't have muscle control yet. Just pick him up and take him outside. Clean the spot with an enzymatic cleaner, which absorbs the odor.

BASIC COMMANDS

SIT

Sit is the first and easiest obedience command to teach your dog. It's also a useful tool in your training toolbox. Once your Collie learns how to sit, incorporate it into everyday life: Sit for dinner; sit while I attach your leash; sit before we go out the door.

You want your dog to lower his rear to the floor and keep it there until you release him. Start by holding a treat slightly above and in front of his head, but not so high that he wants to jump up to get it. Gradually move the treat backward over his head. He'll back up and gradually lower his rear end to the floor. Let him eat the treat while you praise him and he's still in that position. There's no reason to use the word *sit* yet; he has no idea what it means. He needs to learn that he's finished with the exercise, so use a release word. Say, "Okay," to tell him he's done.

Another way to introduce the *sit* is to position your dog sideways in front of you, and gently scoop under his rear with one arm while blocking his forward movement with your other arm across his chest. Reward him when he's in the correct position. This method is especially easy with puppies.

It takes at least three repetitions before the dog starts to understand what's going on. He'll anticipate what you're going to do, and the *sit* will soon come easily. At this point you can add the word. Always praise him and quit when he's made an improvement.

After a few sessions, try having him sit in another location. If you were training in the yard, try it in the living room. You may find he has no idea what you are talking about. He knows what *sit* means in the yard, but until he understands how to sit in the house, on the street, at the store, and when someone else asks him to sit, he doesn't really know the command. This is called generalizing his learning. Once he performs the *sit* nicely everywhere, he really gets it.

COME

Come is probably the most frustrating concept to teach. It's easy for your Collie to associate it with things he doesn't like, and once the word is spoiled, it's harder to retrain. For example, if you call your dog at the park and then hook him up to the leash and put him in the car, he's not going to come next time because he knows the fun is over. Reward him for coming with a short walk or a game of fetch before you take him to the car.

With that in mind, always make something fun happen when your Collie responds to the *come* command. Call out to him in a happy tone, not in a gruff or stern manner. Say, "Come here," and your voice will naturally rise at the end, and your dog will respond better.

Start when your puppy is young and still following you everywhere. Get down on the ground, open your arms wide, and happily call him to you. Use hugs, treats, and toys to reward him for responding. The best reward is to release him immediately to go back to playing. Start teaching up close and gradually call him from farther away. Never get mad at your dog for coming to you slowly. Why would he come if you're just going to yell at him? Start praising and encouraging him as soon as he looks your way. When he gets to you, praise him again.

To establish a reliable *recall*, don't call him if you can't enforce the command. At about four to five months old, your preteen Collie will decide to test you and take off in the opposite direction.

Most obedience commands are taught with the dog right by your side. Paying attention from across the yard or dog park is a new concept for him. When you're ready to practice calling him from a distance, attach a long line so you can reel him in if he ignores you. Add distractions, like other dogs and people, once he is responding well to you. It will take a lot of practice before he learns he has to come even when he has something better to do, like herd those kids over on the soccer field.

STAY

Stay is another useful skill. You'll be able to ask your Collie to stay while you're answering the front door, waiting at the vet's office, or are otherwise occupied. Start with very short-duration (30-second), on leash *sit-stays* and gradually work up to longer durations. It is harder for dogs to hold the *sit* position, so if he's going to be there for a while, ask for a *down-stay*. A well-trained adult dog should be able to hold at least a three-minute *sit-stay* and a 30-minute *down-stay*.

How to Teach *Stay*

Start with your Collie on the leash directly in front of you. Ask for the *sit* and wait a few seconds before you release him with your *okay* word. Give him treats when he's sitting still and not fidgeting. If he starts to get up or lie down, say, "Ack" while stepping near him to stop him. If he does get up or lie down, walk him a few steps on the leash, put him back in the same spot, and start again. If you allow him to move forward and sit, he'll gradually make headway across the room. *Stay* doesn't mean "creep across the floor"; it means "stay right here in this position and don't move." Use the word *stay* with a hand signal: your flat palm perpendicular to his face.

Gradually increase the time he stays, then alternate very short *sit-stays* with longer ones of a minute or more. Praise him and give him treats while he sits. This doesn't mean he can get up—it just means he's doing a good job. Remember to use *okay* when he can get up so that he clearly knows when he's done.

Once you can get him to stay for one minute while you are standing right in front of him, it's time to add some distance. Have him sit on your left side and then step away from him with your right foot. Collies are visually oriented, so he's more likely to follow if you start with your left foot. Turn and face him from about 3 feet (.9 m) away. If he starts to get up, stop him as before and move a little closer.

When you start adding distance, shorten the time he has to stay. It's easier for him to learn one concept at a time. Gradually add distance, and then start to extend the time again. You should be able to walk back to him, give him a treat, and go back to your spot without him moving. As he gets more reliable you can do things like walk around him, pull on the leash so he resists you, walk away with your back to him, and add distractions like bouncing balls. When he has a reliable *stay* in one location, practice in other rooms, outdoors, and during walks. When you see his attention shift to something else, praise him for staying and give him a treat before he has a chance to break the *stay*.

DOWN

Down is a little harder for the dog to do initially, but once he's in position, he is more comfortable holding the *down* longer than the *sit*. One reason dogs resist the *down* is because it is a submissive, vulnerable position. Also, when you stand over him, it lures your Collie up out of the position. If you bend over to talk to your dog, he sees that as an invitation to stand up, so it takes self-control for him to hold the *down*.

How to Teach *Down*

There are several ways to introduce the *down*. For puppies, sit on the floor with one leg bent. Lure the puppy under your leg with a treat. Do this several times, gradually lowering your knee, so the puppy has to duck under your leg to get to the treat. From that you can easily get him to go all the way down as he crawls under your leg. Pair the action with the word "down" when you see him start to lie down automatically. Eventually he will lie down before he goes under your leg, and as you progress, ultimately lie down without your leg there at all. For older Collie puppies, try standing on one knee with the other leg out in front of you, and lure him under that.

Another way to teach the *down* is to have your dog sit while you get down on the ground in front of him. Slowly pull a treat from in front of his nose straight down to the floor. As he dips his head, pull the treat away along the floor. He'll stretch out and lie down as he reaches for it.

Once he understands the command, you can ask him for a *down* from a standing position. It may confuse him if you are standing in front of him rather than at his side, so practice both ways until he understands.

HEEL (WALK NICELY ON A LEASH)

The best way to teach your dog to walk nicely on a leash is to get—and keep—his attention. He won't be dragging you down the street if you're more interesting than his surroundings. Once he knows how to go for a walk, you won't need to be so strict. The term *heel* is a competition obedience word that describes a precise position. The dog walks with his shoulder at the left seam of your pant leg and never lags behind or pulls forward. If you aren't interested in competition obedience, it's okay to use the word "heel" when you mean a looser, less strict position. If you think you'll ever compete, you'll want to choose another term, like "Let's go."

To start, let your puppy or adult Collie drag the leash while you walk briskly around an enclosed yard. Every time he comes to your side, give him a treat. If you have trouble getting his attention, carry a squeaker or toy that you can toss around in your hands. Encourage him to keep up, and make it a game. Turn suddenly, reverse directions, run away, or stop; reward him when he catches up. After a few sessions, try this exercise on leash. Every time he hits the end of the leash, make a sudden turn and reward him for catching up. Once he is used to staying by your side, you can use the "sudden move" method when his attention wanders.

Break up a walk by asking for some *sits*, *downs*, and *stays*, by walking fast or slow, and by allowing some free sniff time. Make the walk interesting and he'll stick closer to your side.

HOW TO FIND A DOG TRAINER

All Collies (and owners) benefit from obedience classes. Besides learning new things or brushing up on existing skills, time spent together improves your relationship with your Collie. The entire family should be allowed to attend, although the trainer may want just one person to handle the dog during class.

How do you find a good trainer? Ask a fellow dog owner for a recommendation. If she lives locally, ask your breeder. If she's not nearby, ask her to refer you to a Collie club member in your area for suggestions. Your veterinarian

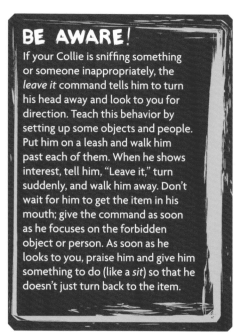

BE AWARE!

If your Collie is sniffing something or someone inappropriately, the *leave it* command tells him to turn his head away and look to you for direction. Teach this behavior by setting up some objects and people. Put him on a leash and walk him past each of them. When he shows interest, tell him, "Leave it," turn suddenly, and walk him away. Don't wait for him to get the item in his mouth; give the command as soon as he focuses on the forbidden object or person. As soon as he looks to you, praise him and give him something to do (like a *sit*) so that he doesn't just turn back to the item.

or pet sitter may have an instructor she recommends. Local kennels may offer training or refer you to an instructor. Your city's park department may also hold classes. An Internet search will unearth some other possibilities.

Once you find an instructor you are interested in, call and ask some questions:

- What methods and equipment does she use—all positive reinforcement, or does she use other methods?
- Is she a member of any dog training clubs or organizations, like the Association of Professional Dog Trainers (APDT)?
- Does she compete in any sports with her dogs?
- What breeds does she own? Has she trained Collies before? What does she think of them? (Walk away from the trainer who says Collies' heads are too narrow to hold a big brain.)
- Will she let you observe a class?

When you watch the obedience class:

- Do the students and dogs seem happy? Are they having fun?
- Do people look like they are successful with their dogs?
- Do the students get individual attention? Are their questions answered?
- If it's a big class, is there an assistant instructor?
- Are the dogs wearing regular collars, or are they wearing prong collars or chain collars? (Prong or chain collars are not appropriate.)

Dog Tale

Bob Weatherwax has trained several generations of Collies who played Lassie and hundreds of other dogs for television, movies, and as pets. When asked if his Collies were easy to train, he replied, "Yes and no. Collies are very smart and were bred to work with the shepherd. They enjoy working with you and at your direction. Once they understand something, they are willing and able. Collies are harder to motivate than other breeds. A ball-crazy Lab will work for a tennis ball; a Collie usually won't. The best motivator I have found for Collies is food, used as a lure and reward. What a German Shepherd will learn in a few hours might take a Collie several days—not because German Shepherds are smarter but because Collies are more methodical and thoughtful. Punishment or other aversive methods ruin a Collie's attitude. Lassie had to look happy as he performed his role. We always used positive reinforcement to train, with the minimum correction necessary. A dog who is forced to obey will be sullen and unhappy. Who wants a dog that does what you want, but with his tail between his legs and his head down in fear?"

CHAPTER 8

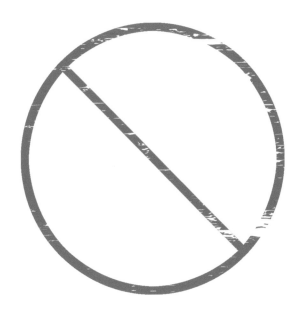

SOLVING PROBLEMS
WITH YOUR COLLIE

After a nonscientific survey of more than 100 Collie owners, I came to the conclusion that Collies have one problem behavior in common: barking. Most people (including me) swear their Collies are perfect and have no behavior issues at all. This is good news for owners, but we all know every dog isn't perfect. Collies, like other dogs, will indulge in doggy behaviors that we don't appreciate, such as chewing, digging, and jumping on people. What we may view as unacceptable is often just typical canine behavior. Part of the solution to these issues is management as well as training.

One of the best ways to prevent problem behaviors is obedience training. Even when you're not working on a specific problem, a dog's overall behavior will improve when he learns the basics of *sit*, *down*, *come*, and *stay*. Your Collie learns to listen to you. He learns that life has rules, structure, and rewards. He learns his place in the home and looks to you for guidance. You exercise his mind as well as his body while building the bond between you. An untrained dog is like an undisciplined teenager—he makes his own rules and runs wild because he doesn't know any better.

With many problem behaviors, you're trying to teach your dog not to bark, jump, etc. These are hazy concepts and are more difficult for your dog to grasp. Instead, teach him alternative acceptable behaviors, like sitting when you see he's going to jump up on someone. Teach him to respond to you and give him something else to do when he does. Let's look at some typical behavior issues from a Collie owner's perspective.

BARKING

We'll never get a Collie to stop barking any more than we can train him to stop eating. Collies use their voice to herd sheep or cattle. They bark at stray sheep to herd them back to the flock. They bark to chase off predators that threaten the herd. Today, pet Collies still take their work seriously, running fence lines and barking at passersby, visitors, and children running around in the backyard.

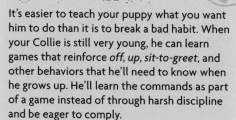

PUPPY POINTER

It's easier to teach your puppy what you want him to do than it is to break a bad habit. When your Collie is still very young, he can learn games that reinforce *off*, *up*, *sit-to-greet*, and other behaviors that he'll need to know when he grows up. He'll learn the commands as part of a game instead of through harsh discipline and be eager to comply.

Because Collies are hardwired to bark, managing your dog's environment will help you control the problem. There are many types of barking, and once you identify why your Collie is barking, you can come up with a management plan. Rather than fix the barking, fix the cause.

If you yell at your Collie to be quiet, he'll just think you're joining in the fun. And does he really know what "quiet" means? When he's barking at you, give it a name like *speak*. (A friend of mine always uses, "What does Lassie say?") When he stops, even for a second, tell him, "Good quiet" and reward him. As you practice, you'll anticipate when he's going to stop and you can give the *quiet* command just before he quits. He'll soon learn what it means.

GREETING

Barking when you arrive home is probably the least offensive type of barking, but your dog may carry it to extremes. Stay calm and ignore your dog until he is calm, too. A low-key arrival on your part will result in a low-key greeting on his part. This will take several weeks of practice before he understands. Quietly reward him for being calm so that he knows this is the behavior you want.

DISTRESS

Your Collie will tell you when a stranger is approaching his territory. Acknowledge his concern and let him know you're taking over now. If he doesn't stop barking, give him something else to do. Have him fetch his toy or do a one-minute *down-stay*.

BOSSY BARKING

Dogs will tell you when it's dinnertime, walk time, or treat time whether you think it is or not. Your Collie will quickly train you to respond to his every command. Try to ignore him until he quits barking, or he'll discover that barking gets him what he wants. Even negative attention is better than no attention in his eyes. If ignoring him doesn't work, put him in his crate for a time-out until he is quiet for a few minutes.

GROUP BARKING

When the entire neighborhood of dogs is calling to each other, sharing the latest news, it's only natural your dog will join the party. If they don't quit in a few minutes, bring your Collie inside.

Collies are hardwired to bark, so you'll need to manage his environment to stop problem barking.

BARRIER BARKING

Barrier barking is usually caused by frustration. Your Collie sees someone walking by and wants to say hi or protect his territory. A territorial dog is rewarded because the passerby leaves—he has successfully chased her away! Barrier barking can quickly turn into a chronic habit that's hard to break. The best cure for this problem is management. Cover a chain-link fence or put up a solid fence to block his view. Close the drapery or keep him out of rooms that face the street.

Teach your dog to leave the object of interest and come to you. Practice the *recall* so that you can call him away from the fence, giving him fabulous treats and attention when he responds. Attach a long line to his collar and have someone walk by the house so you can practice. Reel him in with the line if he ignores you. It's really hard for your Collie to leave such a fun activity, so you need to be extra interesting to make it worth the trouble. Never scold him when he gets to you or he'll be less willing to come next time. You may be seething inside, but you need to reward him for listening.

OBSESSIVE BARKING

A bored Collie will take up recreational barking because he has nothing better to do. Be sure your Collie is getting enough exercise and attention. If you are gone all day at work, spend time with him when you are home. He needs walks, playtime, and time with you to occupy him and wear him out.

Try to keep him occupied while you are away. Stuff some toys with treats and freeze them. Give him one when you leave. Food dispensing toys are also a good way to keep him entertained. Put his breakfast in the toy so it takes him some time to finish eating.

CHASING AND NIPPING

A herding dog chases the flock, nipping at the animals' heels to make them move to where he wants them. Because you probably don't have a herd of pet cows, it's only natural that he'll chase and herd anything that moves when he gets the opportunity. When you find he's cornered the kids in the yard, you'll know you have some retraining to do. A Collie will also chase bicycles, motorcycles, and horses; the movement stimulates his natural instincts so dramatically that he can't help it.

But chasing cars and horses isn't safe. Manage your Collie's behavior by keeping him on leash whenever you take him out of your backyard. When you see him

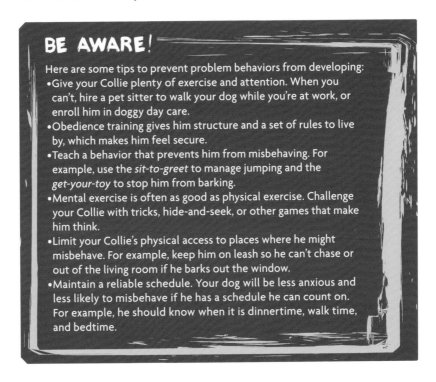

BE AWARE!

Here are some tips to prevent problem behaviors from developing:
- Give your Collie plenty of exercise and attention. When you can't, hire a pet sitter to walk your dog while you're at work, or enroll him in doggy day care.
- Obedience training gives him structure and a set of rules to live by, which makes him feel secure.
- Teach a behavior that prevents him from misbehaving. For example, use the *sit-to-greet* to manage jumping and the *get-your-toy* to stop him from barking.
- Mental exercise is often as good as physical exercise. Challenge your Collie with tricks, hide-and-seek, or other games that make him think.
- Limit your Collie's physical access to places where he might misbehave. For example, keep him on leash so he can't chase or out of the living room if he barks out the window.
- Maintain a reliable schedule. Your dog will be less anxious and less likely to misbehave if he has a schedule he can count on. For example, he should know when it is dinnertime, walk time, and bedtime.

Manage your Collie's herding instincts by redirecting his focus to you.

focusing on a moving object or animal, get his attention back on you by asking for a *sit* or *down*, or do some quick *heels* and about-turns. Don't wait until he's ready to give chase; distract him as soon as you see something has his attention.

At home, when children are running and playing, have mercy on your dog and bring him inside if he's getting too excited. Nipping is as instinctive to a Collie as herding. He'll grab at pant legs and flailing arms with no intention of hurting the kids. Teach the children to "be a tree." Have them stand still and wrap their arms around themselves, turning their backs to the dog. When the dog calms down, they can return to a less lively game. Supervise kids and dogs so that everyone plays safely.

CHEWING

Teenage Collies chew to relieve teething pain. A hard chew toy helps the teeth set in his jaws and relieve the irritation. Other than that, Collies are not typically destructive chewers once they are adults. If your Collie is chewing, look for a reason. Issues like separation anxiety or boredom may make your dog chew. If he is chewing clothes or shoes, it's likely that your scent on them comforts him. Cut off the dog's access to things he's likely to chew. Pick up clothes, shut bedroom doors, or put up pet gates. Spray forbidden objects with bitter apple or another repellant. Give him some appropriate items, like frozen food-stuffed toys and hard rubber bones. Crate him when you aren't able to supervise.

Collies may get into mischief, but at least they have a sense of humor. When my aunt was visiting, I heard her in the other room looking for something. She told me she misplaced her dentures; she swore they were on the nightstand just a few minutes ago. As I walked out of the room, I saw my Collie, Emma, lying in the dining room with a twisted look on her face. When I pried her mouth open, there were auntie's dentures—a little slobbery but undamaged.

DIGGING

Digging is another activity a mischievous teenager or bored adult Collie might engage in. Digging is natural for dogs, although Collies aren't usually fanatics about it. Dogs will bury a bone or scrape out a place to sleep under a bush. If your Collie is digging, is he trying to escape? Put chicken wire along the bottom of the fence to keep him from getting out. If he's digging holes in the lawn, bury his feces in the hole. Placing a piece of chicken wire in the hole is another way to discourage digging.

If your dog sees you gardening, he may dig up the freshly tilled dirt. If you use bone meal on your plants, he'll smell it and think there is food buried there.

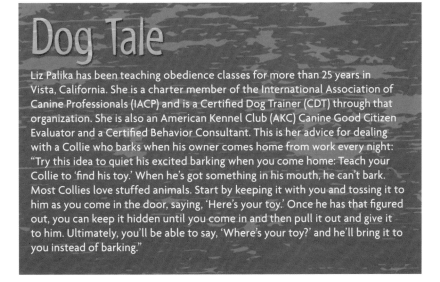

Dog Tale

Liz Palika has been teaching obedience classes for more than 25 years in Vista, California. She is a charter member of the International Association of Canine Professionals (IACP) and is a Certified Dog Trainer (CDT) through that organization. She is also an American Kennel Club (AKC) Canine Good Citizen Evaluator and a Certified Behavior Consultant. This is her advice for dealing with a Collie who barks when his owner comes home from work every night: "Try this idea to quiet his excited barking when you come home: Teach your Collie to 'find his toy.' When he's got something in his mouth, he can't bark. Most Collies love stuffed animals. Start by keeping it with you and tossing it to him as you come in the door, saying, 'Here's your toy.' Once he has that figured out, you can keep it hidden until you come in and then pull it out and give it to him. Ultimately, you'll be able to say, 'Where's your toy?' and he'll bring it to you instead of barking."

A housetrained dog who suddenly starts having accidents may be reacting to stress.

As a last resort, keep your Collie in the house when you can't supervise him, or designate a digging area filled with interesting chew toys.

HOUSE SOILING

Collies should be easy to housetrain and accident-free by four to five months of age. If your Collie is having accidents in the house, there may be a medical reason, like a urinary tract infection. Have your dog examined by a vet, and bring in a urine sample for her to test. Female Collies sometimes suffer from spay incontinence, a condition where they lose muscle control. An inexpensive daily medicine manages this problem. Sometimes the best solution is the most obvious: Does your dog get outside often enough? Put your dog on a regular schedule that he can count on. A fully housetrained dog can go eight to ten hours without an accident, but he would rather not. If you have an unneutered male, especially if he's young, he may be feeling his hormones and need a refresher course in Housetraining 101. If so, constant supervision and more crate time between outdoor trips are in order.

A healthy dog who has been housetrained but suddenly starts having accidents may be reacting to stress. If there has been a major change in the home—someone moving out or in, a major illness, a new pet, or another stressful situation—your Collie may be reacting to your distress or suffering from his own anxiety. Once things settle down, your dog's habits should return to normal. Meanwhile, calming herbs like lavender oil (dabbed on his ear) or Rescue Remedy (a Bach Flower remedy given orally) may relieve some of his anxiety. Limit his access in the house so you can catch him in the act and take him out, just as if you were starting housetraining from the beginning.

The biggest housetraining mistake dog owners can make is to stop going out with their dog too soon. Your Collie may not be quite housetrained and may need more time to get the idea. Praise him and give him a treat every time he potties outdoors. Take him to a preferred spot every time. (If this spot has changed, he may be confused.) Start over with his housetraining routine. Never let your Collie out of your sight when he's in the house, and take him out every two hours. Be sure to clean up accidents with an enzymatic odor remover that completely neutralizes urine odors so that your dog won't think it's okay to return to the scene of the crime.

Make sure you are not accidentally encouraging your Collie to jump up.

If your dog only has accidents at night, pick up his water a few hours before bedtime. Go out with him before bedtime to be sure he relieves himself, and crate him at night.

JUMPING UP

Even though Collies are gentle, you probably still don't want yours jumping up on you. Your dog gets excited and wants to smell your breath and lick your face when he greets you, like a puppy would greet his mother. You inadvertently reward him by touching and talking to him, so he repeats the behavior. Even if you are yelling at him, in the excitement of the moment, he considers any attention to be good attention.

Teach your Collie to sit when greeting you or another person. If he's sitting he can't jump at the same time. When you see your dog is going to jump up, ask for a *sit*. Stand tall and lean into your dog. This makes you more imposing, and your body language tells him not to jump. Praise him calmly when he sits. You'll be more successful if he is calmer. It will take several tries for him to get the idea. In fact, this is a tough lesson because you are working with an excited dog; it may take a number of sessions before he consistently sits for you.

It may take a few training sessions before your Collie consistently sits for you.

Sitting to greet other people is entirely different in his eyes. The person he's focused on is not giving the command. Practice at home and with friends. If he is too excited to sit right in front of them, have him sit a few feet away so he isn't rewarded for breaking the *sit* by being allowed to jump. You'll need to practice in many different places for several weeks before *sit-to-greet* becomes a habit.

Sometimes you may want your Collie to jump on you. Teach him the *up* command by patting your chest and encouraging him to jump up. As he puts his feet back on the floor, say, "Off." *Off* is different from *down*, which he has already learned means to lie down. Don't confuse him by using the same word for two different things.

When you want him off, don't look him in the eye; it encourages him to jump back up. Fold your arms and turn your back on him so that he gets nothing for jumping up. Ignore him until he's got all four feet on the floor. If you manhandle him off of you, you reward him by touching him and with what he sees as play. ("Oh, how fun! She'll wrestle me to the ground!")

WHEN TO SEEK PROFESSIONAL HELP

When your Collie's behavior is driving you crazy, you may need one-on-one help to get it under control. Once a behavior has become a habit, it is self-reinforcing—

in other words, the behavior is so rewarding that it motivates him to continue regardless of your training. And this is where many owners get stuck.

So how do you know when it's time to get help?

• When you feel overwhelmed and don't know how to deal with a problem.
• When you are afraid of your dog.
• If your dog is aggressive, snaps, or has bitten someone.
• If your Collie is overly territorial and protective.
• When your dog won't let you approach his food bowl or toys.
• When you are facing legal action because of your dog's behavior.

Your first step should be a complete veterinary checkup. If your dog is growling when you touch him, for example, he may be in pain. Once medical causes are ruled out, consult with a dog trainer who specializes in problem behaviors. Many obedience instructors teach classes but don't have expertise in more complex issues. Ask for a referral to a qualified expert. Check the Certification Council for Professional Dog Trainers website (www.ccpdt.org) or The Association of Professional Dog Trainers website (www.apdt.com) to find a trainer.

If you need to consult with someone who has more advanced knowledge of dog behavior, there are several organizations that maintain a database of professionals with scientific education and experience. These organizations test and certify their experts:

• **International Association of Animal Behavior Consultants (IAABC):** Members have been tested in major areas of behavioral science and counseling. The IAABC database can help you find either a Certified Animal Behavior Consultant (CABC) or a Certified Dog Behavior Consultant (CDBC) in your area (https://iaabc.org).
• **Animal Behavior Society (ABS):** Certified applied animal behaviorists have a graduate degree in animal behavior and are qualified to diagnose and treat complicated problem behaviors (www.animalbehaviorsociety.org).
• **American College of Veterinary Behaviorists (ACVB):** A veterinarian with the "ACVB" affiliation has completed a residency of one to three years, participated in a behavior research project, and passed a two-day exam. Your veterinarian can refer you to a veterinary behaviorist, who is the only specialist allowed to prescribe medications to treat your Collie's behavior issues (www.dacvb.org).

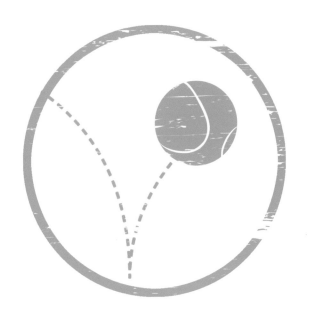

ACTIVITIES WITH YOUR COLLIE

I n this chapter, we'll look at some of the many sports and activities that your entire family can enjoy with your Collie. Also, we'll help you plan for when you want to take your Collie with you on family outings and vacations.

COLLIE SPORTS AND ACTIVITIES

There are many activities, both competitive and noncompetitive, that you can enjoy with your Collie. The American Kennel Club (AKC) and the American Working Collie Association (AWCA) host a number of sports events that welcome Collies, as do other groups described in the sports listed below. If you're not the competitive type, you can attend classes and have fun with your dog without entering shows or trials. If dog sports aren't for you, there are social and volunteer activities in which your entire family can participate.

AGILITY

Agility dogs run an obstacle course with their handler, similar to a jumping course you'd see at a horse show. Collies aren't the speed demons that Border Collies or terriers are, but even a slower dog–handler team can qualify for ribbons and titles. If your dog runs without faults and within the time limit, you qualify. Faults include knocking down a jump or failing to hit contact points (marked areas) on certain obstacles. Dogs compete according to their height. Courses range from beginner courses that include jumps only to jumps and weave poles to courses with more difficult obstacles.

AKC CANINE GOOD CITIZEN PROGRAM

The Canine Good Citizen (CGC) Program promotes well-behaved dogs and their owners at home and in public. Your Collie demonstrates his good manners

There are many competitive and noncompetitive activities for your Collie.

during a ten-step evaluation, while you sign a pledge to be a responsible pet owner. When he passes you get a CGC certificate from the AKC.

Many obedience instructors use the CGC program as the basis for their classes and incorporate the test into graduation. Pet therapy groups and 4H organizations also incorporate the CGC test into their training.

The CGC is made up of ten tests that a dog must successfully complete:

1. Accept a friendly stranger who approaches and speaks to the owner
2. Sit politely for petting by a stranger.
3. Accept grooming and handling by a stranger, and present in a clean, healthy, and well-groomed condition.
4. Walk nicely on a leash at the owner's side.
5. Walk through a crowd under control without excessive shyness or resentment toward strangers.
6. Sit and lie down on command and stay in place while the handler walks 20 feet (6 m) away and returns.
7. Come when called.
8. Demonstrate a polite reaction to another dog while owners greet each other and walk together.
9. Demonstrate confidence when faced with a distracting or mildly upsetting situation, such as someone dropping a chair or rolling a cart past the dog.
10. Tolerate separation from his owner, without becoming overanxious, while someone else holds the leash.

BARN HUNTS

Barn hunts are exciting for both the dog and handler. Your Collie follows a scent through straw bales to find a hidden rat at the end (in a protected, aerated tube). As your dog advances through the levels, the tests get more complicated, and he has more time to find the rat. He can earn titles that are recognized by the AKC. Visit the Barn Hunt Association at www. barnhunt.com.

PUPPY POINTER

Some owners start scent tracking with their Collies while they wait for their puppy to mature enough to jump safely in agility or participate in obedience. Puppies can start tracking as young as 12 to 16 weeks old, although they can't compete until six months of age. In other sports, puppies can't start training until they're at least one year old, when their bones have matured and they are less likely to be injured while running or jumping.

CARTING

Carting involves hooking your Collie up to a small cart or wagon that he pulls at your command. Once he gets the hang of it, he'll be a big hit at parades and other public activities. If you have a healthy, athletic Collie, he may enjoy this sport. The AWCA offers working titles to Collies in backpacking, wilderness, and carting venues.

CONFORMATION

When you see Collies competing at a show like the Westminster Kennel Club Dog Show or the AKC/Eukanuba National Championship, these dogs are competing in conformation. Dogs are judged by how closely they "conform" to the ideal standard of the Collie as set forth by the Collie Club of America (CCA). Dogs are evaluated on structure, temperament, and movement. In breed competitions, dogs compete by sex, age, and other divisions. The top dog in each class competes against champion Collies for the Best of Breed award. In a Collie specialty show, where only Collies are competing, this is the top award.

In an all-breed show, the best-of-breed Collie competes in the Herding Group against the best-of-breed German Shepherd Dog, Shetland Sheepdog, Australian

In conformation, dogs are evaluated on structure, temperament, and movement.

Shepherd, Corgi, and other herding breeds. The Herding Group winner goes on to compete for Best in Show against the other group winners from the Sporting, Terrier, Working, Nonsporting, Hound, and Toy groups.

HERDING

Herding trials give your Collie the opportunity to demonstrate that he has the skills the breed was developed to perform. Dogs work with ducks, sheep, or cattle and can earn titles through several organizations. Most programs offer beginner tests for novice handlers.

Collies were traditionally used to herd all types of livestock, and they exhibit a variety of herding styles. They are considered "soft" herders, as compared to a Border Collie, who eagle-eyes his flock into submission. The typical Collie excels at gathering stock and bringing it to the shepherd. Others work best as drovers, pushing the stock down a road, for instance.

The CCA offers a Herding Instinct Test for Collies six months or older. The test introduces Collies and their handlers to basic herding, and although both you and your dog may have no herding experience at all, you can see if your Collie instinctively tries to move the sheep. An experienced stockdog trainer handles your dog, who is evaluated for his interest in the livestock. If he circles the flock or follows as if to drive it, he passes the test and earns a Herding Instinct Certificate.

The AKC offers several levels of beginner tests, including the Herding Instinct Test, Herding Test (HT), and Herding Pre-Trial Test (PT). In each, the judge evaluates the dog's ability to move and control livestock according to predefined standards. Your Collie may then move up to actual trials, which offer Starter, Intermediate, Advanced, and Champion titles. To earn titles, dogs must perform certain skills in each trial, and they receive a title after a designated number of qualifying runs.

The Australian Shepherd Club of America (ASCA) offers a stockdog program that welcomes all herding breeds. The ASCA awards titles and also gives owners the opportunity to participate in novice and "for exhibition only" tests.

The American Herding Breed Association (AHBA) offers Herding Trial Dog (HTD) and Herding Ranch Dog (HRD) titles. The AHBA also offers beginning herding tests: the Herding Capability Test (HCT) and Junior Herding Dog Test (JHD), where handlers and dogs get a pass or no pass score and earn their title after two passing runs under different judges.

The AWCA conducts herding tests and also accepts titles from other organizations toward their Versatility titles.

NOSE WORK

One of the newest activities in canine sports is nose work. While some people train their dogs for search and rescue, tracking titles, arson detection, and more serious forms of scent work, pet owners came up with nose work as a way to have some lighthearted fun with their canine buddies. In this activity, handlers train their dogs to search for their favorite treats and toys. All you need is a motivated dog and his favorite reward, whether it is food or a toy.

Scent challenges get progressively harder as your dog builds his skills and learns the game. Your Collie gets to burn off energy, build his confidence, and best of all, spend time with you. Like so many other organized dog sports, there is a national association, training workshops, and trials where your dog can earn nose work titles. One of these is the National Association of Canine Nose Work (NACSW).

OBEDIENCE

The AKC developed obedience trials to showcase well-behaved dogs. There are three title levels: Novice, Open, and Utility. The Novice class exercises include basic obedience skills that you teach your dog in everyday life: to heel on leash and off, sit, sit-stay, down, down-stay, come, and stand for examination by another person (the judge). The exercises get progressively more difficult as the dog advances through the classes. More advanced title requirements include retrieving over a jump, heeling, dropping on *recall*, broad jumping, and longer *stays*.

When a dog achieves a qualifying score in three trials under two different judges, he earns a Companion Dog (CD) title for the Novice class, a Companion Dog Excellent (CDX) for the Open class, and a Utility Dog (UD) title for the Utility class. Dogs can go on to earn Utility Dog Excellent (UDX), Obedience Trial Champion (OTCH), and National Obedience Champion (NOC) titles.

RALLY OBEDIENCE

Traditional AKC obedience trials include precise movements and are very competitive. Rally obedience was developed to offer owners a more relaxing way to show their dogs. The handler takes her dog through a course of 10 to 20 stations and performs an obedience exercise at each one. The handler–dog team works at its own pace, and the handler is encouraged to talk to and praise her dog along the way.

There are three levels of Rally: Novice, Advanced, and Excellent, and dogs earn titles in each category after earning three qualifying scores under two different judges.

Activities are available for both beginners and seasoned competitors.

SEARCH AND RESCUE

Collies were considered excellent search and rescue dogs in World War I because they would find an injured soldier and continue barking until help arrived. It was difficult to train other breeds to do this. Today, many breeds volunteer with their owners for local and national search dog organizations, not just for the military.

Search and rescue requires an extremely focused team that can find specific scents amid extreme conditions without getting distracted. You both must be well trained and available at a moment's notice when called to help. Teams always work hand-in-hand with law enforcement.

TRACKING

We picture the mighty Bloodhound tracking an escaped prisoner through a swamp when we think about tracking, but all breeds have an exceptional sense of smell. The Collie is no exception. Tracking tests allow your dog to demonstrate his ability to follow a human scent and find "lost" articles of clothing—like a glove— along the way. Tracking used to be part of the utility obedience competition, but today dogs earn the titles separately.

Unlike the other sports that require three qualifying outings, a dog earns his tracking title after one successful track in the AKC. The levels are Tracking Dog (TD), Tracking Dog Excellent (TDX), and Variable Surface Tracking (VST).

ACTIVITIES WITH YOUR COLLIE

125

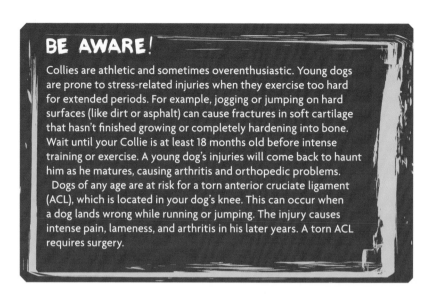

BE AWARE!

Collies are athletic and sometimes overenthusiastic. Young dogs are prone to stress-related injuries when they exercise too hard for extended periods. For example, jogging or jumping on hard surfaces (like dirt or asphalt) can cause fractures in soft cartilage that hasn't finished growing or completely hardening into bone. Wait until your Collie is at least 18 months old before intense training or exercise. A young dog's injuries will come back to haunt him as he matures, causing arthritis and orthopedic problems.

Dogs of any age are at risk for a torn anterior cruciate ligament (ACL), which is located in your dog's knee. This can occur when a dog lands wrong while running or jumping. The injury causes intense pain, lameness, and arthritis in his later years. A torn ACL requires surgery.

For a TD, the dog must follow a track 30 minutes to 2 hours old and over 440 to 500 yards (402 to 457 m) long. When he moves up to the TDX level, he must follow a track three to five hours old that is 800 to 1,000 yards (732 to 914 m) long. VST dogs track a scent in an urban setting rather than in the wilderness, so they track over asphalt and grass and through buildings. A dog who has earned all three titles becomes a Champion Tracker (CT).

ACTIVITIES FOR CHILDREN

Your children can participate in the sports listed above, but there are also canine activities they can do on their own:

- **4H:** Your local county cooperative extension offers 4H programs for children (www.4-h.org). Activities vary, but kids can train their dog and compete in obedience, agility, grooming, handling, and more. Kids also learn to keep records and care for their dog's health while competing at local and state fairs.
- **Scouting:** Boy Scouts and Girl Scouts of all ages can earn badges in pet care and responsible dog ownership while also learning about wild animals, veterinary hospitals, and other pet-related activities.
- **Junior showmanship:** Children 9 to 18 years old can compete in AKC junior programs. The Conformation Junior Showmanship Class has been available to kids for many years. The AKC has recently introduced programs recognizing juniors in obedience, agility, and tracking.

- **Animal shelters:** Many shelters offer summer camp programs where kids can learn about animals and interact with them.

SOCIAL ACTIVITIES WITH YOUR COLLIE

DOG CLUBS

The CCA is the AKC parent club for the Collie, and there are local Collie clubs throughout the United States. Although most of the members compete in conformation, they also participate in other Collie activities, like picnics and fun matches. If you are interested in showing Collies, attend a few shows and talk to your breeder to learn more about it. If your children are interested in showing in conformation, they can train and compete in junior handling classes and shows.

Besides breed clubs, there are all-breed agility, obedience, nose work, tracking, and other dog groups you can join.

DOG PARKS

Visits to your local dog park offer your Collie the socialization and exercise he needs. Go without your dog first to see how your dog park operates. The busiest times are evenings and weekends. Be sure you're comfortable that your Collie will be safe. There is usually no supervision, so owners are on their own. Some owners

Visits to your local dog park offer your Collie the socialization and exercise he needs.

don't pay any attention to their dogs, who then bully others and start fights. If you find that your Collie doesn't enjoy the roughhousing and commotion, leave. Some dogs just don't care for dog parks.

RESCUE VOLUNTEERING

Collie rescue groups all over the country work hard to help homeless Collies. The volunteers also have a lot of fun and become great friends. Even if you're unable to foster a dog or can't bear to visit shelters, there are many ways you can help. Work in an adoption booth at a street fair, write articles, help with fundraising, or attend Collie outreach activities.

THERAPY VISITS

Collies make wonderful therapy dogs. Our breed is universally loved, and so many people in nursing homes and other facilities have special memories of Collies from their childhood. Collie owners visit schools, rehabilitation hospitals, nursing homes, and day care centers to share their beloved dogs with others. With more advanced training, your Collie can participate in actual therapy sessions with patients.

Dogs who go on visits must be certified through a therapy dog organization to ensure the safety of those being visited. You can attend classes to prepare your dog for certification. Dogs will be exposed to things they may not have seen before, like a wheelchair or walker. You will both learn special commands to use during visits. You'll learn about cleanliness and safety procedures, and your dog will be temperament tested, possibly with the CGC test.

Dog Tale

Jean Levitt is president of the American Working Collie Association (AWCA) and has a Collie assistance dog named Tucker. For beginners interested in getting involved with AWCA activities, she says, "The AWCA offers programs in carting, backpacking, herding, obedience, agility, scent work, and more. They developed a versatility title program in which dogs earn titles for participating in a variety of activities. The AWCA either offers its own titles in a category or accepts other programs' titles as credit toward the versatility titles. This is a noncompetitive group that has a coordinator for each category and mentors newcomers in the activity of their choice. The group welcomes novice members and feels time spent enjoying your Collie is the most important goal."

Pet Partners (https://petpartners.org) and Therapy Dogs International (www.tdi-dog.org) offer certification on a nationwide basis. Local chapters, obedience instructors, and therapy groups may offer training classes. Pet Partners also offers online classes that help you prepare for therapy visits.

WALK-A-THONS AND OTHER SOCIAL GROUPS

Humane societies, fundraising groups, and schools often hold walk-a-thons, where you sign up sponsors and walk for a cause. There are also meet-up groups, fitness groups, and yoga clubs that cater to dog owners. Once you start looking, you'll find endless possibilities for dog-friendly social outings.

TRAVELING WITH YOUR COLLIE

Do some advance research before taking a trip with your Collie. Once you understand state regulations and hotel, campground, and airline policies, you'll find dog-friendly accommodations at most tourist destinations.

Before you travel, prepare with the following:

- **Health certificate:** Visit your veterinarian before you take your dog across state lines. You'll need to carry a health certificate and vaccination records. A current rabies vaccine is required, and other vaccine requirements vary by state. Usually, the health certificate must be issued no more than seven to ten days prior to departure.
- **Identification:** Microchip and tag your dog with identification before your trip. Dogs traveling internationally should have a microchip that meets International Organization for Standardization (ISO) standards, which is an internationally recognized frequency. Add the microchip number to your Collie's health certificate. Include your cell phone number or an alternate contact number on your Collie's ID tag.
- **Heartworm preventive:** In most areas of the country, your Collie will be exposed to the risk of heartworm infection. If your dog is not already on a heartworm preventive, have him tested and start the preventive before you leave.

TRAVEL CHECKLIST

Here's a handy checklist of all the items you'll need to travel with your Collie:

- **Bedding, toys, and chews:** Bedding that smells like home will comfort him. Chews or toys will keep him occupied.
- **Cleanup supplies:** Be a good citizen and ensure that dogs continue to be welcomed in public places. Bring disposable poop bags and paper towels.

- **Crate:** Make sure that your dog is acclimated to the crate before you travel.
- **First-aid kit:** Your kit should include a long strip of gauze for wrapping injuries or muzzling a frightened dog, tweezers to remove thorns or stingers, antihistamine (like Benadryl) in case of a bee sting, sanitary pads to bandage a bleeding wound, blunt-nosed and pointed scissors, elastic bandages, antiseptic solution, gauze pads, a pet first-aid book (or smartphone app), and the phone number of the closest emergency vet.
- **Food, treats, and bowls:** You may not be able to find the same brand of food at your destination, so carry some with you to prevent stomach upset.
- **Health certificate:** If you are flying or crossing state lines, this is required.
- **Leash:** Always leash your Collie in public, especially in an unfamiliar place.
- **Microchip information:** Bring the chip number, registry name, and contact information. Take a photo of your dog with you.
- **Water:** Water from an unfamiliar place can cause diarrhea. Bring your own or buy bottled water.

TRAVELING BY CAR

The safest place in the car for your dog is in a crate. Why restrain your dog? Any kind of unruly behavior in a car is dangerous. The passing cars stimulate his herding instinct, and he may jump around and bark out the windows. He could hit the stick shift, smack you in the face with his tail, or cause some other safety hazard. A nervous dog in an unfamiliar place may rush out and run away when you open the car door.

Tie the crate down so that it won't fall over when you go around corners. If your car isn't large enough for a crate, teach your dog to wear a harness attached to the seat belt. There are specially made car harnesses for pets, or you can make one. Have him ride in the backseat so that he won't be injured by the airbag if you're in an accident. Don't let your Collie hang out the window while you drive; debris can injure his eyes.

Rest areas can be hazardous places for a dog. Keep your Collie on leash so that he doesn't encounter a snake or get into discarded food. Be a responsible dog owner and clean up after your dog.

Carsickness

Take your Collie on some short, fun rides before a long trip to get him used to car travel. Stress and the car's motion might make him carsick. Symptoms include drooling, trembling, a hunched back, and retching or vomiting. To combat carsickness, lower the windows about an inch (2.5 cm) to equalize the air pressure

in the car. Ginger is a natural treatment for nausea. Open a capsule of ginger and pour it onto some food or yogurt. A ginger snap cookie may help settle his stomach. Limit his food and water at least an hour before travel. Play calm music and give him a favorite toy.

Heat Is Dangerous

The most common cause of heatstroke in dogs is being left in a car. It can get too hot for your dog in less than five minutes, even in relatively cool weather. Once overheated, the dog quickly gets dehydrated and goes into shock. Cracking the windows and parking in the shade is not enough to keep him safe. If your Collie is confined in a crate in the back of the minivan, check to be sure he is getting enough air and that the sun isn't directly on him, even while the car is moving.

TRAVELING BY AIR

If you want to ship your Collie by air, consider the risks. Although airlines take precautions, your dog will be shipped as cargo. In the cargo hold, temperatures can fluctuate wildly, and your dog may be exposed to flight delays that risk his health and safety. With more than 2 million dogs being transported each year, the airlines have an excellent safety record, but you won't be able to monitor your pet every minute, and dogs have been known to escape, be permanently lost, or die in transit.

Do some advance research on travel safety before taking your Collie on a trip.

Call the airline directly to book your dog's flight; most carriers don't allow online pet reservations. Airlines also set limits on the number of animals they will take on any given flight. Most airlines have travel regulations for pets posted on their websites. Always reconfirm with the airline 24 to 48 hours before you leave. Shipping a large dog can be pricey; a ticket for your Collie may cost as much as your seat.

If you are traveling on an international flight, check with the country you are visiting, because there may be long periods of quarantine at your destination. Even Hawaii has strict guidelines for bringing animals to the islands.

Try to book a nonstop flight, and avoid holiday or weekend travel so that your dog doesn't have to switch planes. Check the weather forecast, too. Many airlines ban flying with animals when the ground temperature is too high or too low. Overnight flights are a good alternative if you are flying with your dog in the summer.

Most vets recommend against sedating your Collie before flying. Besides the fact that some Collies are known to have an adverse reaction to acepromazine (a commonly prescribed tranquilizer), sedatives can affect your dog's equilibrium and ability to regulate his temperature. A fully awake dog is usually safer.

Airline-Approved Crate

If your Collie isn't crate trained, take the time to do so before your trip so that he'll feel safe rather than stressed when crated. Your crate must be Food and Drug Administration (FDA) and Federal Aviation Administration (FAA) approved and conform to the individual airline's regulations. The crate must be sturdy, properly ventilated, and large enough that he can stand, turn around, and lie down. Clearly display your name and address on the kennel, and use arrows or stickers to indicate the top of the kennel.

Secure empty food and water dishes inside the crate door so that they are accessible from the outside. Attach a food and water schedule, and if any food is necessary, include it in a bag taped to the outside of the kennel.

Airline Security

In this age of added security screenings, your Collie and his crate will be subject to security inspection just like any other passenger. The Transportation Security Administration (TSA) will have you remove your dog from his crate and will inspect the kennel using the same security procedures as carry-on or checked baggage.

PET-FRIENDLY LODGING

Plan in advance to stay at pet-friendly hotels and campgrounds when you travel. Most have a limited number of rooms available for dog owners, so make advance reservations. Some hotels have size limits for their canine guests and charge an extra daily fee. Others designate their smoking rooms as dog-friendly rooms. Major chains like Holiday Inn, Motel 6, and Best Western accept dogs. Some facilities offer extra amenities for dog owners, like dog day care, play yards, dog walkers, and treats.

Dogs are allowed in most national parks, but they must be kept in your car or in the parking lot and aren't allowed on hiking trails at all. Some parks have one or two trails designated for dogs, and many have dog-friendly national forests nearby.

RESOURCES

ASSOCIATIONS AND ORGANIZATIONS

BREED CLUBS

American Kennel Club (AKC)
8051 Arco Corporate Drive, Suite 100
Raleigh, NC 27617-3390
Telephone: (919) 233-9767
E-mail: info@akc.org
www.akc.org

American Working Collie Association
26695 Snell Lane
Los Altos Hills, CA 94022
Telephone: (650) 941-1022
E-mail: jocollie@att.net
www.awca.net

Canadian Kennel Club (CKC)
200 Ronson Drive, Suite 400
Etobicoke, Ontario M9W 5Z9
Telephone: (416) 675-5511
Fax: (416) 675-6506
E-mail: information@ckc.ca
www.ckc.ca

Fédération Cynologique Internationale (FCI)
FCI Office
Place Albert 1er, 13
B-6530 Thuin
Belgique
Telephone: +32 71 59.12.38
Fax: +32 71 59.22.29
www.fci.be

The Kennel Club (UK)
Telephone: 01296 318540
Fax: 020 7518 1058
www.thekennelclub.org.uk

Collie Club of America (CCA)
Telephone: (785) 983-4894
E-mail: secretary@ collieclubofamerica.org
www.collieclubofamerica.org

Collie Rescue Foundation, Inc. (CRF)
E-mail: crfmembership@yahoo.com
www.collierescuefoundation.net

The Collie Association (UK)
Telephone: 01202 891146 07774 579386
E-mail: janfred.clynelish@fsmail.net
www.collieassociation.co.uk

United Kennel Club (UKC)
100 E. Kilgore Road
Kalamazoo, MI 49002-5584
Telephone: (269) 343-9020
Fax: (269) 343-7037
www.ukcdogs.com

PET SITTERS

National Association of Professional Pet Sitters (NAPPS)
1120 Route 73, Suite 200
Mount Laurel, New Jersey 08054
Telephone: (856) 439-0324
Fax: (856) 439-0525
E-mail: napps@petsitters.org
www.petsitters.org

Pet Sitters International (PSI)
Telephone: (336) 983-9222
E-mail: info@petsit.com
www.petsit.com

RESCUE ORGANIZATIONS AND ANIMAL WELFARE GROUPS

American Humane Association
1400 16th Street NW, Suite 360
Washington, DC 20036
Telephone: (800) 227-4645
E-mail: info@americanhumane.org
www.americanhumane.org

American Society for the Prevention of Cruelty to Animals (ASPCA)
424 E. 92nd Street
New York, NY 10128-6804
Telephone: (212) 876-7700
www.aspca.org

Royal Society for the Prevention of Cruelty to Animals (RSPCA)
RSPCA Advice Team
Wilberforce Way
Southwater
Horsham
West Sussex
RH13 9RS
United Kingdom
www.rspca.org.uk

SPORTS

International Agility Link (IAL)
85 Blackwall Road
Chuwar, Queensland
Australia 4306www.
lowchensaustralia.com/shows/
international-agility-link.htm

North American Dog Agility Council (NADAC)
24605 Dodds Road
Bend, Oregon 97701
www.nadac.com

North American Flyball Association (NAFA)
1333 West Devon Avenue, #512
Chicago, IL 60660
Telephone: (800) 318-6312
Fax: (800) 318-6312
E-mail: flyball@flyball.org
www.flyball.org

United States Dog Agility Association (USDAA)
PO Box 850955
Richardson, TX 75085
Telephone: (972) 487-2200
Fax: (972) 231-9700
www.usdaa.com

World Canine Freestyle Organization (WCFO)
4547 Bedford Avenue
Brooklyn, NY 11235
Telephone: (718) 332-8336
E-mail: wcfodogs@aol.com
www.worldcaninefreestyle.org

THERAPY
Alliance of Therapy Dogs (ATD)
PO Box 20227
Cheyenne, WY 82003
Telephone: (877) 843-7364
Fax: (307) 638-2079
E-mail: therapydogsinc@
qwestoffice.net
www.therapydogs.com

Pet Partners
875 124th Ave NE, #101
Bellevue, WA 98005
Telephone: (425) 679-5500
www.petpartners.org

Therapy Dogs International (TDI)
88 Bartley Road
Flanders, NJ 07836
Telephone: (973) 252-9800
Fax: (973) 252-7171
E-mail: tdi@gti.net
www.tdi-dog.org

TRAINING
American College of Veterinary Behaviorists (ACVB)
College of Veterinary Medicine, 4474 TAMU
Texas A&M University
College Station, Texas 77843-4474
www.dacvb.org

American Kennel Club Canine Health Foundation (CHF)
PO Box 900061
Raleigh, NC 27675
Telephone: (888) 682-9696
Fax: (919) 334-4011
www.akcchf.org

Animal Behavior Society (ABS)
2111 Chestnut Ave, Suite 145
Glenview, IL 60025
Telephone: (312) 893-6585
Fax: (312) 896-5619
E-mail: info@
animalbehaviorsociety.org
www.animalbehaviorsociety.org

Association of Professional Dog Trainers (APDT)
2365 Harrodsburg Road A325
Lexington, KY 40504
Telephone: (800) 738-3647
Fax: (864) 331-0767
https://apdt.com

Certification Council for Professional Dog Trainers (CCPDT)
Professional Testing Corporation
1350 Broadway, 17th Floor
New York, NY 10018
Telephone: (855) 362-3784
E-mail: administrator@ccpdt.org
www.ccpdt.org

International Association of Animal Behavior Consultants (IAABC)
565 Callery Road
Cranberry Township, PA 16066
www.iaabc.org

National Association of Dog Obedience Instructors (NADOI)
7910 Picador Drive
Houston, TX 77083-4918
Telephone: (972) 296-1196
E-mail: info@nadoi.org
www.nadoi.org

VETERINARY AND HEALTH RESOURCES
Academy of Veterinary Homeopathy (AVH)
PO Box 232282
Leucadia, CA 92023-2282
Telephone: (866) 652-1590
Fax: (866) 652-1590
www.theavh.org

American Academy of Veterinary Acupuncture (AAVA)
PO Box 803
Fayetteville, TN 37334
Telephone: (931) 438-0238
Fax: (931) 433-6289
www.aava.org

American Animal Hospital Association (AAHA)
12575 W. Bayaud Ave
Lakewood, CO 80228-2021
Telephone: (303) 986-2800
Fax: (303) 986-1700
E-mail: info@aaha.org
www.aaha.org

American College of Veterinary Internal Medicine (ACVIM)
1997 Wadsworth Boulevard
Lakewood, CO 80214-5293
Telephone: (303) 231-9933
Telephone (US or Canada): (800) 245-9081
Fax: (303) 231-0880
E-mail: ACVIM@ACVIM.org
www.acvim.org

American College of Veterinary Ophthalmologists (ACVO)
PO Box 1311
Meridian, ID 83680
Telephone: (208) 466-7624
Fax: (208) 466-7693
E-mail: office15@acvo.org
www.acvo.org

American Heartworm Society (AHS)
PO Box 8266
Wilmington, DE 19803-8266
E-mail: info@heartwormsociety.org
www.heartwormsociety.org

American Holistic Veterinary Medical Association (AHVMA)
33 Kensington Parkway
Abingdon, MD 21009
Telephone: (410) 569-0795
Fax: (410) 569-2346
E-mail: office@ahvma.org
www.ahvma.org

American Veterinary Medical Association (AVMA)
1931 North Meacham Road, Suite 100
Schaumburg, IL 60173-4360
Telephone: (800) 248-2862
Fax: (847) 925-1329
www.avma.org

ASPCA Animal Poison Control
Telephone: (888) 426-4435
www.aspca.org/pet-care/animal-poison-control

British Veterinary Association (BVA)
7 Mansfield Street
London
W1G 9NQ
United Kingdom
Telephone: 020 7636 6541
Fax: 020 7908 6349
E-mail: bvahq@bva.co.uk
www.bva.co.uk

Orthopedic Foundation for Animals (OFA)
2300 E. Nifong Boulevard
Columbia, MO 65201-3806
Telephone: (573) 442-0418
Fax: (573) 875-5073
E-mail: ofa@offa.org
www.offa.org

US Food and Drug Administration Center for Veterinary Medicine (CVM)
US Food and Drug Administration
Communications Staff (HFV-12)
7519 Standish Place
Rockville, MD 20855
Telephone: (240) 402-7002
E-mail: AskCVM@fda.hhs.gov
www.fda.gov/AnimalVeterinary/

PUBLICATIONS
BOOKS
Adamson, Eve, with Sandy Roth. *Complete Guide to Dog Grooming*. Animal Planet. Neptune City: TFH Publications, Inc., 2011.

Anderson, Teoti. *Dog Training*. Animal Planet. Neptune City: TFH Publications, Inc., 2014.

Kennedy, Stacy. *Complete Guide to Puppy Care*. Animal Planet. Neptune City: TFH Publications, Inc., 2000.

King, Trish. *Parenting Your Dog*. Neptune City: TFH Publications, Inc., 2010.

MAGAZINES
AKC Family Dog
American Kennel Club
260 Madison Avenue
New York, NY 10016
www.akc.org/pubs/family-dog/

AKC Gazette
American Kennel Club
260 Madison Avenue
New York, NY 10016
www.akc.org/pubs/gazette/

WEBSITES
Nylabone
www.nylabone.com

TFH Publications, Inc.
www.tfh.com

INDEX

Page numbers in **bold** typeface indicate a photograph.

PHOTO CREDITS:

DEDICATION

This book is dedicated to the volunteers and supporters of Southland Collie Rescue in honor of the wonderful work you do for homeless Collies.

AKCNOWLEDGMENTS

Thanks to the many breeders, rescuers, and Collie lovers for providing many of the wonderful photos used in this book. Thank you also to the many people who helped me in my research for this book, including Gayle Kaye, Bob Weatherwax, Janet Merriman, Monique Guerin, Liz Palika, Don Ironside, Julie Sandoval, and Jean Levitt.

ABOUT THE AUTHOR

Terry Albert is an award-winning writer and artist specializing in pet-related subjects. She has had hands-on experience with many breeds of dogs as a professional dog trainer, foster, and professional pet sitter. She has owned several Collies and fostered numerous Collies for Southland Collie Rescue over the years. When she lived in Seattle, she served as the Collie Breed Rep for Seattle Purebred Dog Rescue. In addition, Terry has served on the Board of Directors for Seattle Purebred Dog Rescue and the Humane Society of Seattle/King County.

Terry is also known for her paintings of dogs. Her artwork has been exhibited at the "Art Show at the Dog Show" in Wichita, Kansas, and the American Kennel Club Museum of the Dog. She currently works from her home, which she shares with two dogs, four horses, and two cats.

ABOUT ANIMAL PLANET™

Animal Planet™ is the only television network dedicated exclusively to the connection between humans and animals. The network brings people of all ages together by tapping into our fundamental fascination with animals through an array of fresh programming that includes humor, competition, drama, and spectacle from the animal kingdom.

ABOUT *DOGS 101*

The most comprehensive—and most endearing—dog encyclopedia on television, *DOGS 101* spotlights the adorable, the feisty and the unexpected. A wide-ranging rundown of everyone's favorite dog breeds—from the Dalmatian to Xoloitzcuintli —this series surveys a variety of breeds for their behavioral quirks, genetic history, most famous examples and wildest trivia. Learn which dogs are best for urban living and which would be the best fit for your family. Using a mix of animal experts, pop-culture footage and stylized dog photography, *DOGS 101* is an unprecedented look at man's best friend.

At Animal Planet,
we're committed to providing
quality products designed to
help your pets live long,
healthy, and happy lives.